Adventure Dogs

Adventure Dogs

ACTIVITIES TO SHARE WITH YOUR DOG FROM COMFY COUCHES TO MOUNTAIN TOPS

Fern Watt

CHRONICLE BOOKS

SAN FRANCISCO

For Rosey, Kruze, Yoda, Gizelle, Nala, Bertha, Oscar, Mopdog, and Bette.

PREVIOUS PAGE: Elsa, Bailey, Jeanie, Titch, Dolly, and Vince.

Library of Congress Cataloging-in-Publication data is available.

ISBN 978-1-7972-0783-4

Manufactured in India.

Design by Jon Glick

FRONT COVER PHOTOGRAPHY BY (TOP LEFT, CLOCKWISE): Courtney Dasher, Jamie Sun, Jim Zelasko, Rosa Gjurkowitsch, Seth Casteel, and Cherie Molloy.

BACK COVER PHOTOGRAPHY BY Andres Monasterios and Natalie Sanchez.

10 9 8 7 6 5 4 3 2 1

Chronicle books and gifts are available at special quantity discounts to corporations, professional associations, literacy programs, and other organizations. For details and discount information, please contact our premiums department at corporatesales@chroniclebooks.com or at 1-800-759-0190.

Chronicle Books LLC
680 Second Street
San Francisco, California 94107
www.chroniclebooks.com

"84 DOG

"~~Twenty~~ years from now you will be more

disappointed by the things you didn't do (WITH ME)

than by the ones you did do.

So throw ~~off~~ the ~~bowlines~~ BALL!!!

~~Sail~~ LEAP OFF ~~away from~~ the ~~safe harbor~~ SOFA!

Catch the ~~trade~~ winds in your ~~sails~~ NOSE!

Explore! Dream! Discover!" SQUIRREL?

~~—Mark Twain~~
—MY DOG BETTE

Contents

Foreword

By Seth Casteel

My name is Seth Casteel, but most people know me as the "Underwater Dogs" guy. I first met Fern on the "Raining Cats and Dogs" panel at the *L.A. Times* Festival of Books where we had the opportunity to speak about our experiences as authors of dog books (while holding umbrellas). We instantly became friends because of our shared love of

dogs. There were also a few cat people on the panel, whom we had to further evaluate before befriending them, but they turned out to be awesome as well.

As an underwater dog photographer, I spend a lot of time with canines in the pool. This might sound repetitive. It's not. It's incredible and often surprising to watch dogs leap from the ledge and splash into the water after their favorite toy. Most people assume that because I work with dogs who enjoy swimming and retrieving, I must be surrounded by golden retrievers and labs all day. But I've seen Maltese and Chihuahuas go bananas in the pool, and labs bolt at the sight of a small splash. I met a Dachshund named

Rhoda who always avoided the pool in her backyard. One day, her human decided to teach her how to get out of the water, in the event she ever accidentally slipped in. As it turned out, Rhoda *loved* to swim, and it became her number one hobby! She even taught herself how to knock her own ball in and dive down *six feet* to retrieve it. It's exciting and always inspiring to watch dogs overcome their fears and learn how to do new things. You never know what hidden talents or amazing instincts your dog might be waiting to release if presented with the right opportunity.

So, when Fern told me her new book, *Adventure Dogs*, was filled with incredible activities and experiences for dogs to try,

I was really excited for the lucky canines out there about to experience something new. The book is a road map to all of the most amazing dog adventures—from herding to howling to pulling to playing exciting games in the living room to yes, jumping in the pool in the backyard! My philosophy with working with dogs has always been to do what they want to do. Follow them on their adventures and, while they are in the middle of being the best version of themselves, you may have a chance to capture a glimpse of their world This book provides a lot of opportunities for dogs to become their best selves. And as you watch your dog enjoying life a little more, I'm certain you will, too.

I'm always looking for more ways to enjoy life with my best pal Nala, a rescue poodle mix from Southern California. Nala is more of a "retirement community" dog at this point and her regularly scheduled programming includes sleeping, relaxing, tinkling, snacking, and staying in air-conditioned (72° F) spaces. But there are, of course, terrific adventures for her in these pages, too. Nala has attempted to "graduate from the Ivy League." She's gone on a very stimulating "smell walk" around the neighborhood. And we are still trying to come up with a Guinness World Record to set that combines one of her favorite things (squirrels) with one of my favorite things (margaritas). Let us know if you come up with something, would you?

Whether you have a senior bulldog or a new Labrador puppy, one of the best parts of having a dog in your life is to enjoy a great friendship. And what do friends do? They do things together! The world is an exciting place—now go experience it. And may your dog's nose be your guide.

Introduction

Greetings, dog people! If you picked up this book, you likely do not need me to convince you that life is more fun with your dog by your side. You're probably already on the lookout for "dogs welcome" signs wherever you go—new places, adventures, and experiences meant to be shared with your most loyal companion. Well, let this book be a flashing neon arrow calling all breeds, sizes, dispositions, and personalities to join in on the fun.

Today, there are more households with dogs than children. Sometimes I swear that Bette, my complex, mischievous, thirty-pound little baby, *is* a furry human. But Bette is a cattle-dog mix, bred to hunt and bark and drive livestock. She's my best friend, but *(newsflash, Fernie, I know)* she's not a person. I want to make her life as fulfilled and full of joy as possible. But how? What do *dogs* want to do for fun?

That VERY philosophical question is exactly what I asked myself when setting out to write this book. I've always wondered whether there was more to my dog's joy menu than sticks, balls, and squirrels. So, I made it my mission to give my dog the best life ever. Bette learned to sniff for truffles, summited new mountains, and ran a canicross race! We ate treats, took a road trip across two countries, and even went to herding school. I also reached out to an impressive array of canine experts—dog behaviorists, scientists, Navy SEAL trainers, best selling authors, and owners just like you—to find the very best ways for humans to understand, appreciate, and live life to the fullest with their four-legged friends.

From the bulldog whose idea of a hike is the ten steps from her bed to her bowl to the Border collie who attempts to herd humans in the living room, there are adventures for all types of pups (and people) in these pages. Some are location specific, and others are perfect for your own backyard. Whether you are going on a "smell walk" around the neighborhood, nailing a dance move, or finally setting off on that epic cross-country car ride, each activity will strengthen the connection you share with your dog.

JRR Tolkien said, "It's no bad thing to celebrate a simple life," and I hope this book is a reminder of that. I hope this book inspires you to get around to those big adventures, but to also make more time for the ones within reach. The more time I spend with my dog, the more I am reminded that sticks are not just fallen tree branches but high-quality entertainment! I've discovered that the dog park is more fun to watch than anything on TV and that a well-exercised animal is a happy one. I've learned that dogs don't always benefit from living more like

us. We benefit from living more like them. Human years move fast. Dog years move faster. Taking your dog on new adventures is a great way to take yourself on new adventures.

So, grab your pooch, and let's have an adventure, shall we?

1
Wanna Go for a Walk?

I love exploring the world on foot with my dog, but this does not mean "Take a long walk with Bette," always makes it to the top of my to-do list. Sure, on busy days, I *try* to convince myself that the ten hurried steps Bette and I race from the front door to the closest, dinkiest patch of grass counts as "a walk." But, when it comes to strutting your mutt, it's best to think beyond potty breaks.

Regular walks of twenty minutes or more have tons of health benefits for your pooch (and for you!). Walking the dog can be a high point in your day, a chance to take a break from the TV, meet the neighbors, or check out the suburban wildlife *(Is that a squirrel?!)*. When we take our dogs on longer walks, we give them a chance to explore the world. Whether your stroll takes you five miles up a majestic trail or just to the end of a new street, walks help deepen the emotional bond we share with our pets. There are thousands of paths just waiting for you and your dog to explore. Ready? Let's go!

OPPOSITE: Tucker, Hera, Coque, Sokee, Tara, and Little.

Go for a Smell Walk

WITH HELP FROM ALEXANDRA HOROWITZ, *NEW YORK TIMES* BESTSELLING AUTHOR
AND LEADING RESEARCHER IN DOG COGNITION

There are pack walks and "go potty!" walks, run walks, and short walks. But for your pup's olfactory experience, none of those come close to the excitement and spontaneity of Alexandra Horowitz's "smell walk."

"Taking your dog for a 'smell walk' is a great way to enrich their daily lives," suggests Dr. Horowitz, author of *Being a Dog: Following the Dog into a World of Smell* and head of the Horowitz Dog Cognition Lab at Barnard College. "A smell walk is simply a walk where you let the dog stop and sniff whatever they choose. It's not a fast walk. It's a walk at dog-pace—maybe lingering at a tree trunk for three minutes and then racing over to an invisible smell on a fence. It's following the dog."

Bette's walks tend to feel more like a game of tug-of-war where I am pulling left, and she is pulling towards, well, whatever invisible smells are not to the left. "To pull a dog away from a smell is like having a door slammed in your face when you simply start *looking* at something," Horowitz explained. "A smell walk is not intuitive for many owners because as visual creatures, we don't initially see what all the fuss is about. Why do they stick their nose in *everything*? Well, it turns out that is their way of seeing, and that is their world. We need to slow down and let dogs sniff."

According to Horowitz, a smell walk should not be timed, and there is no end destination or route. It's going wherever your dog's nose desires. "The smell walk is defined precisely by how long and how much my dogs can sniff in," Horowitz says. *Uh-oh.* I thought. *Does my dog have a limit to how much she can sniff in?* Ready to find out, I grabbed a jacket, gloves, and a few other provisions (Did I need food? Water? A headlamp?) to follow wherever Bette's nose took us.

McConkey and
Salix Sully

At first, this was not far. Bette stopped to sniff our mailbox so intensely I began to wonder whether we'd ever leave the driveway. *Well, at least smell walking is easy.* Then Bette saw a squirrel, and the smell walk turned into a smell run.

The squirrel darted up a tree, and Bette zigzagged down the sidewalk, stopping to sniff bushes, trash cans, droppings, dirt, fresh grass, dead grass, sticks, and our four-legged neighbors butt *(oh, hey Huey!)*. I did my best to keep up with her and practiced patience as she explored. It was nice to go for a walk without an agenda—to be spontaneous and leave the direction up to Bette.

Soon we reached a crossroads, and Bette looked at me confused, waiting for me to tell her where I wanted to go. I could almost feel her delight as she realized that *she* got to choose. She really could follow her nose!

COME TO YOUR SENSES

Even though dogs have bigger systems to process odors (humans have about six million olfactory receptors; dogs have around 300 million), this does not mean your schnozz should sit the smell walk out. To better relate to how your canine understands the world, Horowitz recommends we start sniffing! While we often limit our perceptions to what we can see, a dog can sniff a beagle on the breeze three blocks up, the bacon the passerby ate for breakfast, the trace of a squirrel on the ground. What can you smell if you pay more attention? Grass? Lavender? Sweat? Springtime? Is that *sniff sniff* barbecue? Shall we eat?

Jimmy

Go for a Pack Walk

WITH HELP FROM TRAINERS ANDRES MONASTERIOS AND NATALIE SANCHEZ, @BARKHAUS

A pack walk typically consists of five to twenty canines being walked at the same time by one or two alpha humans (a.k.a. pack leaders). To normal humans, walking one dog can be difficult. Andres Monasterios and Natalie Sanchez can walk up to forty-two at one time.

Pack-walk leaders are experienced trainers who know how to establish themselves as the alpha within a pack of dogs. At Barkhaus, a canine training facility and adventure camp in Honolulu, walks and hikes can vary between three and ten miles, depending on the needs of the pack. A pack walk has the opposite mentality of the smell walk, but can be even more beneficial, especially for anxious or aggressive dogs. In a pack walk, there is no pulling, no excessive marking, no barking, and no jumping. And absolutely no chasing any squirrels.

But that doesn't mean it isn't any fun for the dogs. "On a pack walk, dogs are able to relax, because they know whoever is handling them is in charge and has their best interest in mind. They are confident and don't have to react to things," says Sanchez, the alpha female of Barkhaus. "Dogs can follow the group and just keep moving forward."

Most behavioral issues in dogs happen for two reasons: The dog is not getting enough exercise and the dog has no idea who is in charge. A pack walk solves both of these problems. As descendants of wolves, dogs are born into the world as pack animals, and they come out of the womb knowing *someone* has got to be the leader. Once your dog moves into your house, that someone should be you! However, *some* of us may struggle to convince our dogs that we are confident

FRONT ROW: Maila, Appa, Brisket, Coconut, Bourbon, Izzy, Noah; **BACK ROW:** Maddie, Obi, Stella, Bo.

Kina, Thunder, Obi-Wan, Izzy, Stella, Sokee, Noah, Abby, Appa, Maddie, Maila, Izzy, Booker

alphas with everything under control (because, like, what if we don't have everything under control?), so the *dog* feels the need to take on that role.

A pack walk allows dogs time with a confident alpha who will give them the leadership that every dog deserves. There's no need to curate a pack walk by size or breed—it's all about energy. Chihuahuas and mastiffs, Great Danes and dachshunds—they can all walk together. "As soon as you start giving your dog the right leadership and the right amount of exercise, behavioral issues disappear," says Sanchez. "Plus, a tired dog is a good dog."

A perfect pack

Walk in the World's Largest Dog Walk

Grab your poop bags and leashes! The Great North Dog Walk set the Guinness World Record on June 12, 2011, for the most dogs to ever go for a single walk. An astounding 22,742 dogs representing 182 breeds walked along the beautiful coastal cliffs of South Shields, England, for three miles. The walk has taken place for nearly thirty years and has raised more than ten million dollars for charitable causes.

CAN'T TRAVEL TO THE WORLD'S LARGEST DOG WALK?

With a quick Internet search, you can find amazing walking clubs and canine social groups right outside your own front door. From breed-specific hikes to socially distanced strolls for shy dogs, these walks might not qualify as the "world's largest," but your dog will still be VERY excited. Here are a few popular canine social groups you could join, or that might inspire you to start your own.

🐾 CORGI CON

Over a thousand Corgis take over a San Francisco beach for a day of playing, agility courses, competitions, and lots of smiling humans.

🐾 THE ADVENTUREWEINER CLUB

Started by influencer and Dachshund expert Jessica Williams (page 70), this club brings Dachshund lovers of western Washington together for playtime, hiking, and socializing.

🐾 INDYHUMANE'S MUTT STRUTT

Hundreds of humans and canines walk the Indianapolis Motor Speedway. There's less speed than the Indy 500, but a lot more belly rubs.

Bubba, Buttons, and Maki gearing up for Corgi Con

🐾 THE POSITIVE PITTIE PACK WALK

A walking group open to all dogs in Hoboken, New Jersey, aims to improve the image of the pit bull breed.

🐾 "DINOS" (DOGS IN NEED OF SPACE)

The group doesn't meet for obvious reasons, but the online community is a reminder to everyone that less sociable dogs (DINOS) are still good dogs.

Go for a *Reeeeaaally* Long Walk

WITH HELP FROM ADELE NG AND WHISKEY THE VIZSLA, @MYWHISKEYGIRL

For the dog who can't get enough of the words "Wanna go for a walk?" could there be anything more exciting than a multi day, pack your kibbles, overnight hike? You'll need to prepare a lot more than poop bags for this type of trek—food, water, bowls, tent, backpacks, treats, first aid, maps, and more—and do your research first. Some common questions to ask include: Do I need a permit? Is the trail dog-friendly? Should I train? Will there be bears? And, of course, there are rules you and your pet must follow if you want to safely become guests in a wild animal's home.

Adele Ng, a professional photographer and avid outdoor adventurer, and Whiskey, her purebred Vizsla and very best friend, live in British Columbia, a place filled with dog-friendly trails to explore. One of Adele's most memorable walks was a five-day trip through Mount Edziza Provincial Park in northern British Columbia, a place so remote the duo had to take a floatplane to reach it. Whiskey and Adele scrambled up mountain passes, crossed roaring rivers, and climbed waterfalls with two other human companions. There are no roads in this part of the world. No marked trails. No amenities or shelter. But the rewards for choosing the path less traveled (or maybe not traveled at all) are amazing. Spot real-deal wildlife well beyond the squirrel, dine under the stars with a crackling fire and your best friend, cozy up in a sleeping bag with the serenade of the back country night dwellers, then wake up with the first rays of sunshine and say those magic words again:*Wanna go for a walk?* And hopefully, fingers crossed, you still do!

Whiskey in Mount Edziza Provincial Park

"Whiskey reminds me to go out constantly, no matter the weather. Sometimes the best adventures happen when everyone else is at home." —Adele Ng

Walk on the Beach

Going to the beach with my first dog, an English mastiff named Gizelle, was a relaxing activity. We would sit, stroll, listen to the waves, watch surfers, and enjoy the tranquility of being where the land meets the sea. Going to the beach with Bette, on the other hand, involves a lot more cardio. Bette runs, splashes, jumps, chases, swims, and digs (yes, digging is actually encouraged here)!

While any dog-friendly beach nearby is a win, there are amazing beach destinations for dogs across the country and around the world. If you're looking for a day trip or a reason to pack your cute beach outfits and make a vacation of it, just remember that salt crusted on your skin and seawater in your hair is even *better* with your pooch by your side!

🐾 THE ORIGINAL DOG BEACH,
SAN DIEGO, CALIFORNIA

One of the first official leash-free beaches in the United States, this landmark is the perfect place to play fetch, or chase seagulls (those pesky seagulls—turns out they're even more elusive than those darn squirrels).

🐾 ROSIE'S DOG BEACH,
LONG BEACH, CALIFORNIA

Head to Los Angeles County's most popular dog beach for a leash-free walk on the Southern California coastline.

🐾 CARMEL BEACH,
CARMEL, CALIFORNIA

After your walk, stop for treats at Terry's Lounge, an iconic 1920s hotel where well-behaved canines can occasionally lounge inside the bar.

Milow and Pablo

 CANNON BEACH,
CANNON BEACH, OREGON
Low tides mean wide beaches, and wide beaches mean more space for running! Play fetch with a fabulous piece of driftwood or snap a picture in front of the famous Haystack Rock.

CASWELL BEACH,
CASWELL BEACH, NORTH CAROLINA
The beach is quiet, the town is sleepy, and it's the perfect place for an afternoon walk with your best friend.

MONTROSE DOG BEACH,
CHICAGO, ILLINOIS
Chicago's first legal off-leash beach allows four-legged friends to dip their paws in Lake Michigan and take a break from city life.

MANSION BEACH,
BLOCK ISLAND, RHODE ISLAND
Take a free Block Island ferry ride and reach this quiet, secluded beach with powdery sand and big waves.

DOG BEACH PARK,
FORT MYERS BEACH, FLORIDA
Splash in the shallow Florida water, dig a hole in the fluffy sand, or go for a kayak ride.

2
Sports
Let's Run! Play! Swim! Pull! Jump!

Sure, you might look at your bulldog snoring like a freight train at three in the afternoon and assume his athletic prowess is limited to propelling his portly body from the floor to the bed (which is, after all, quite a feat). Or that the only determination your pug has involves staring at your plate of food. But, the veterinarians and dog trainers (and doctors and therapists) are right—*all* animals need exercise every day.

Remember, your pooch doesn't have to become the next Air Bud. (And you do not have to be the next Lebron.) There's a reason we call it *playing* sports. It's playing! And we could all stand to do a little more playing. So, pick up a Frisbee, enter a canicross race, or strap on some skis. You and your canine could have tons of hidden talents just waiting to be explored. Today seems like a great day to find out, doesn't it?

Go Backcountry Snowboarding

WITH HELP FROM KELLY LUND AND LOKI THE WOLF DOG, @LOKI

As they reach the summit of the mountain the thermometer reads -6 degrees Fahrenheit, but neither dog nor man is cold. The steep upward climb, paired with the excitement of the adventure to come, provide all the warmth they need. As they arrive at the top, they survey their world: a boundless vista blanketed in white snow, unmarked by human tracks. Kelly Lund edges his board slightly downhill, gives Loki an encouraging nod, Ready boy?

The duo launch into their glorious descent! Lund plows through the pristine Colorado powder and Loki bounds down the mountain behind him. Tongue hanging, snow flying, nothing can compare to the feeling of blasting through knee-deep snow with your best friend. While commercial ski resorts do not allow dogs, humans and canines who are well-trained and skilled enough to navigate the backcountry can experience the thrill of skiing and snowboarding, together.

"The snow is something that Loki was made for, and it's really cool to bring him into his element," says Lund, a photographer, author, animal lover, and outdoorsman who documents Loki's adventures on Instagram for their two million followers. Loki is a low-content wolf dog (meaning he is part wolf, but more dog than wolf). His thick coat, huge paws, and athleticism make him a natural fit for the backcountry. Seeing photos of Loki in the wild it's hard to imagine he could ever be content chewing on squeaky toys or walking on a leash. He looks regal yet comfortable, at home in the coldest, snowiest of places. He's the perfect adventure companion for Lund, who has been chasing backcountry powder for most of his life.

Lund says the best way to hike up the mountain is with a split board, which is

Loki

34

a snowboard that splits into two cross country-style skis for maximum efficiency on the trek up and then is reconnected for maximum thrills on the way down. He doesn't recommend attaching a pack or any extra weight to your dog on skiing adventures. Trekking up a mountain in deep snow is exhausting enough, and your dog could get overworked. For humans interested in this type of extreme adventure, it's crucial to enroll in avalanche-safety training and to be confident skiing or snowboarding the advanced runs at a resort on all types of terrain. People can be trained to read the mountain and not trigger avalanches; canines cannot. When venturing into the backcountry with a dog, stick to slopes that are not steep, where there is little to no avalanche danger. Only a small fraction of terrain is flat enough for dogs to run on and also steep enough to ride or ski. While Lund makes it look easy,

it's important to keep safety in mind at all times.

Lund's mission has always been to watch Loki closely and try to live more like him, instead of the other way around. "Loki reminds me to not overthink adventures too much. To just be out there, appreciating them."

For many of us, trekking up a treacherous mountain to chase backcountry powder might not be our number one priority (I mean, we can't all be Kelly and Loki), but most dogs might enjoy chasing a snowball at least once in their lifetime. Has your dog ever played in the snow? Have you? How about taking your pooch on a non-backcountry snow outing? Build a snow dog! Play a game of chase-the-sled! Make snow doggy angels! Play fetch with snowballs! Who knew there could be a fun side to that foot of white powder on the car? This frigid white stuff is a blast!

Learn to Mush

WITH HELP FROM JENNIFER RAFFAELI, KENNEL MANAGER AND LEAD MUSHER
AT DENALI NATIONAL PARK AND PRESERVE

From the moment the team of sled dogs see their harnesses, yelps and yips, and barks echo through the air. Paws pounce with excitement. *3-2-1 Mush!* Lines pull tight, and the dog-powered sled blasts through the snow into whiteout blizzards and sub zero temperatures. For mushers, the work is not making the sled dogs run. The work is making the dogs pace.

Few animals can run faster and longer than sled dogs. If the Alaskan husky were entering a marathon, he or she could cross the finish line in less than an hour and a half. Unlike humans, these dogs do not run for medals or money or even treats. They run because they love to run. The running *is* the treat! "They do it all for the pure joy of doing, not for some higher cause or great reward, but just because they love the doing," says Jennifer Raffaeli, kennel manager and lead musher of Denali National Park and Preserve.

The Alaskan husky has an impressive résumé for a career as a sled dog. They have the stamina to run hundreds of miles, tough feet to handle ice, thick coats for shaking off the snow, and strength to pull hundreds of pounds behind them. While Bette and I have a hard time *walking* without tangling the leash or pulling in opposite directions, sled dogs work with their musher and canine teammates like a well-oiled machine.

One of the most intuitive and important members of a sled team is the lead dog. The lead dog is the first to plunge across an icy stream, navigate a blizzard, and set the pace for the other dogs. The lead dog must execute the musher's commands, but also have the confidence to break those commands if they know they will lead the team into trouble. Raffaeli says that a great lead dog has a blend of independent confidence and connection to

Disco and Cupcake,
the lead dogs

the musher. "It is something that you can nurture in a dog that has it, but you can't train it into a dog that isn't born with that special ability," she noted.

This made sense. Becoming *any* member of a sled dog team sounded like it required talents, coordination, teamwork and a level of blizzard tolerance most animals weren't born with. Just as I was about to assume that mushing was clearly out of the question for me and my dog, but still a really cool activity for the sled dogs in Alaska, I stumbled upon another "mushing" sport I'd never even heard of: canicross.

Run a Canicross Race

"No, no, no pulling!" For Bette, this was all she used to hear. Me yelling at her to stop pulling on the leash (while, ironically, I am also pulling the leash). I always thought pulling was a bad thing, until I discovered canicross.

Canicross combines trail running and dog sledding. It's basically the easiest way to let your dog pull like she is trying to win the Iditarod, but without the blizzards and frostbite and toboggans and stuff. All you need is a running belt, a harness for your dog, a specialty bungee leash, and a canine with a desire to run. I ordered the supplies, tethered myself to my little Togo-in-training, and was pulled down the sidewalk before I could even shout *Mush!*

With normal leashes, runs with my dog felt more like a game of tug-of-war. With the canicross leash and running belt, Bette could pull without jarring me, and I could run hands-free! Bette and I ran up hills, around lakes, and over streams. If I slowed down, she helped me speed up, just like a real sled team! *Could we be budding canicross champions?*

Ready to find out, I signed up for our first canicross race, a 10K event called Running with the Bears, held in rural, farm-filled Greenville, California.

We stood side by side at the starting line. Dogs howled while humans sang the National Anthem. "OK, five seconds," the announcer yelled. I gave Bette a few pats on the head, trying to calm any pre-race jitters. *We got this, girl!* "Three, two, one . . . mush!"

Farms were a new variable for Bette, and during the first mile, I was seriously concerned that we would never finish if Bette kept slowing down to bark at nearby horses *Yes, I know, we don't see those in LA and yes, I get it, you think they smell very interesting (hmm, I'm picking up something there, too. They do smell interesting! What is that, hay, hibiscus, clover?)—but we've got to focus!!! Stay in the game—one foot in front of the other. Or two feet in front of the other two feet, or however, you do it—but let's go!!* By mile four, the line was pulled tight, and our feet and paws were working together. *We were working together!* Sure, there was no snow. No fancy sled or

41

pristine Alaskan wilderness or blizzards to brave. But running with Bette, I couldn't help but feel like we were channeling our inner sled dogs. We were running not to cross the finish line or reach a distance or time goal or even earn a medal. We were running for the joy of it, Bette's tongue dangled from her mouth and a huge smile spread across my face. We crossed the finish line in roughly thirty-fifth place, but that was the best thing about a dog race. Thirty-fifth felt just like first!

Go Skijoring

So, you survived canicross (or maybe you're just jumping ahead—which is perfectly permissible) and you're ready to "get tangled up" with your four-legged pal in a winter wonderland. Consider skijoring! Skijoring is a Norwegian word that means "ski driving." Like canicross, dogs are tethered to their humans by a six- to ten-foot towline. Unlike canicross, their humans are wearing skis. The dog runs and pulls, and the human skis behind. Easy! (At least, that's what I thought.)

Of course, *some* dogs might need help learning that the skis are not to be chased, in spite of their uncanny resemblance to sticks. And some *humans* might need reminding that they should actually know how to cross-country ski *before* attaching themselves to a very fast and excited four-legged teammate. But with a little practice, patience, and maybe a few tumbles, this sport is a thrilling way to explore the snowy outdoors with your best friend.

LEFT: Twigs and Huck

RIGHT: Ice

Go Bikejoring

Now that you've knocked out cani-cross and skijoring (or again, perhaps you're one of those people who likes to jump to the advanced level), it's time for bikejoring! Bikejoring is similar to skijoring, but instead of being towed by your dog on soft, fluffy, forgiving snow, you're being towed down a rocky, heavily squirrel populated trail at full speed on a *bike!* Sound like an accident waiting to happen? *whispers quietly* It totally is! Bikejoring requires you to surrender physical control of your dog. Yes, humans must replace physical guidance with verbal guidance. Shout "gee" to tell your dog to pull right and "haw" to command her left. More importantly, canines should know the command for stop, which is "woah!"

Before your first excursion, you must ensure that everything you want your dog to do while you're zipping downhill is understood while you still have two feet on the ground. Once you and your four-legged friend have mastered the commands, hop on the saddle for a ride that will change your life. Hang on, and don't forget your helmet!

Mint

47

Become a SUP Pup

WITH HELP FROM JACK AND SAMANTHA EASTBURN, SUP PUPS SAN DIEGO, @SUP_PUPS

Imagine paddling across a beautiful lake with your best pal, watching the afternoon sun glisten off the water. Or what if you could cruise across a calm turquoise lagoon at sunset, peering into little tide pools of fish? Stand-up paddleboarding is a popular aquatic sport that combines elements of surfing and canoeing. But unlike surfing, stand-up paddleboarding doesn't require waves. So, almost anyone can learn to do it, including your dog.

At first, I had some doubts. I was certain my dog and I would be excellent at *fall-off* paddleboarding. But stand-up paddleboarding? I envisioned Bette and I splashing in the water, clinging to the board in a Jack-and-Rose-from-the-Titanic type of situation.

Samantha Eastburn, a stand-up paddleboard instructor and founder of SUP pups San Diego, reassured me that she has trained hundreds of dogs and their humans to stand-up paddleboard together. At SUP Pups, Eastburn and her trusty mutt, Jack, inspire all types of dogs and humans to venture away from the comfort of the shore. She says students are always surprised to discover they can not only learn how to stand-up paddleboard themselves; they can also do it with their furry first mate! Eastburn encourages dogs and humans of all sizes, ages, and athletic abilities to grab a board (and lifejackets) and give it a go. She even helps anxious pups and people overcome water anxiety!

The coolest thing about this sport is that when it comes to water activities, stand-up paddleboarding is one of the easiest to learn with some of the greatest rewards: 360 degree views of the water, a bird's eye view of the fish, and yup, you can B.Y.O.Dog. It helps to learn to paddle when Mother Nature is feeling agreeable—so practice on water that is generally mild, with little to no boat wake, in low wind. Also, make sure your board is big enough for the both of you (at least eleven feet long).

Of course, it's not uncommon for maiden voyages to feel a little wobbly, but most humans and canines find their sea legs during their inaugural class.

Captain Jack (bottom left) and his fellow sea dogs

48

Chase Your Flying Human

WITH HELP FROM ANDREW MUSE AND KICKER DOG, @KICKERDOGMUSE

"**As Kicker's athleticism** has substantially outgrown mine, I've had to get creative on how I take him for walks. I literally have to fly now to keep up with him," says Andrew Muse of his "paragliding" dog, Kicker. A golden retriever, Kicker is the ultimate adventure companion to Muse, an avid outdoorsman, world traveler, producer, Instagram influencer, athlete, and all-around badass.

Kicker and Muse live life on a full-time car ride, traveling the world in an expedition vehicle Muse built, affectionately known as "The Muse Roamer." Kicker has floated down glacial lakes in a packraft and explored ice caves in Alaska, but one of his more noteworthy adventures was paragliding. Kicker flew tandem as a puppy using a climbing-grade dog harness as well as a tandem-paragliding harness, so he could sit, look out, and enjoy the smells. "But I do not recommend flying with your dog unless you have professional training and are at a very advanced level," warns Muse.

Now that Kicker is full grown, he enjoys flying down *hills* on his own four paws, chasing after Muse from below as he soars through the air like a bird. "He's hyped up the minute he sees my wing come out," says Muse. Paragliding is a sport growing in popularity, and it took Muse two weeks of lessons and practicing every day to get the hang of it. "But it's really a lifelong learning process," he explains. "Point of the Mountain in Draper, Utah, is the most dog-friendly place I've found, and a great place for learning. It's a nice gentle, grassy hill. A lot of people bring their dogs, and it's one of Kicker's favorite places to socialize!"

Andrew and Kicker take flight together.

Compete in Dock Jumping

Dogs have always loved jumping off wooden docks to fetch sticks. Now, high-tech camera systems and judges can rank how well they do it! What was once a lazy afternoon activity is now a competitive sport for canines. All you need is a float-able toy and a dog obsessed with retrieving it, and you have yourself a dock jumper.

DockDogs, the organization responsible for bringing this extreme canine aquatic sport to life, hosts multiday events where dogs run and jump from a dock into a pool. The premise might sound simple, but the practice is not. There are handbooks, rules, points tables, Titles, rankings, and judges! Unsurprisingly, there are also different disciplines. Big Air is the most popular; it measures which dog can jump the farthest distance. Humans play an important role in this event because it's up to them to throw the toy and initiate the jump. Extreme Vertical measures how high your dog can jump, and Speed Retrieve races your canine against the clock to see which dog can swim and fetch a thrown object the fastest. Dueling Dogs challenges two canines and their humans to side-by-side racing. To race in Dueling Dogs, two bumpers are suspended in the air above a pool of water. On a *release* command, the canines dash down their race lanes, leap from the ledge, sail their tails into the air , and try to grab the bumper. *Splash!* The dog that grabs a bumper first, wins.

Dock jumping is not limited to retrievers. Over the years, many breeds have achieved dock-jumping glory, from world-record-breaking whippets to high-flying Great Dane mixes to rescue mutts. DockDogs even offers a "lap dog" division for dogs that measure less than seventeen inches from their withers to the ground and a "legends" division for senior dogs.

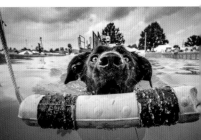

Learn to Surf

Have you ever wondered whether your dog might want to shred more than her favorite toy? Once a year, four-legged surfer dudes paddle into the waves of Huntington Beach, California, for the annual Surf City Surf Dog competition. Canines as small as teacup Chihuahuas and as large as pit bulls have been spotted surfing some sweet waves on the California coast. At Huntington Beach, surfurs—yes, sur*furs*—are scored on their top two waves and can compete in several classes, including solo surfurs and two-dog or dog-human tandems.

"I really think Bono loves the feeling of dropping into a wave with the wind on his face. The same feeling the humans love about surfing!" says Ivan Moreira, human to Bono the surfing brown Lab (@bonosurfdog).

Most dogs ride a foam board, but some fierce competitors, like Sugar (@sugarthesurfingdog), ride custom short boards. "She's like a rocket!" says her human, Ryan Rustan, who found Sugar when they were both living on the streets in Oakland. Sugar has won multiple championships and ridden some of the biggest waves ever surfed by a dog, but those accomplishments pale to Sugar's greatest achievement. Through surfing, Sugar helped Rustan overcome his battle with addiction and homelessness.

Now, I know what you might be thinking. Do *dogs* actually enjoy surfing? Is this activity only for human entertainment? At SurfDog competitions, there are rules that ensure the safety and happiness of two and four-legged athletes, including a strict "no forced surfing" policy. Dogs must actually want to follow their humans into the water. (And they do, in fact, follow their humans right into the water!) I guess some dogs really do want to do everything with their people, and that includes bobbing in the ocean, waiting patiently for that perfect wave.

Sugar and Ryan Rustan

Train Like a Navy SEAL

With help from Mike Ritland, former US Navy SEAL, trainer of the most highly skilled K9 Warriors, and *New York Times* bestselling author of *Team Dog: How to Train Your Dog—The Navy SEAL Way*, @MRITLAND

They chase down terrorists at Zero Bark Thirty, sniff out explosives, parachute into deployment zones, and have prey drives unmatched by man or machine. These are not your average house pets; these are the elite warrior canines of the US Navy SEALs, and Mike Ritland trains them. "The most important thing a SEAL dog demonstrates is heart," says Ritland. "They've got to be willing to give it everything they have. Most dogs, when given a fight-or-flight opportunity where it's paramount that their life is in danger, they will flee that environment. With a good SEAL dog, they won't. They will push harder, fight even harder, and that's an incredibly elusive trait in all animals, humans included."

SEAL dogs are typically Belgian Malinois or German shepherds and must endure training that matches the intensity of human SEALs. While my dog crumbles at the sight of Chihuahuas and vacuum cleaners, potential SEAL dogs must be able to swim far enough to lose sight of the shore, jump in and out of helicopters, and keep their cool around the most alarming sounds—thunder, gunfire, sirens, roaring engines, and explosions. Like humans, it's rare for a dog to possess the physical and mental toughness to become a Navy SEAL. However, Ritland says that with a little leadership, confidence, and proper body language, any civilian can train their own special canine unit the SEAL way.

BE THE TEAM LEADER

Whether you are training a Malinois to charge into a battlefield or training Wiggles to stop chewing the furniture, the principles do not change. If you want your dog to take you seriously, you need to establish yourself as the leader.

"Dogs respect confidence, power, and authority. And by dogs, I mean all dogs," writes Ritland. "I don't care how much of an alpha role any dog has assumed; when someone comes in and exhibits those traits to a greater degree than they do, they will step aside. Mastering your voice and your body in interacting with dogs to project confidence, power, and authority is absolutely essential to the Navy SEAL way."

USE NONVERBAL COMMUNICATION

One of the biggest mistakes people make with dogs is assuming that they understand English. This made sense. I talk to my dog so much you'd think I was under the illusion she might one day speak back. "Everybody thinks that dogs view the world through a human perspective," Ritland explains. "Dogs don't think in a language." When Bette barks because someone rang the doorbell and I yell to stop barking at the doorbell, she most likely thinks I am just as upset as she is about this puzzling, mysterious doorbell thing. So, she will continue barking in solidarity! Ritland emphasized the need to practice emotional stability and never raise your voice when communicating with your dog.

ESTABLISH LOYALTY

Gaining your dog's loyalty isn't about spoiling them with endless toys and treats. It's about working with your dog physically and mentally, taking them on walks, and proving to them that you are a reliable leader worthy of their trust and affection. The more I try to prove to Bette that I am a confident, in control, emotionally stable leader, the more I actually *become* a confident, in control, emotionally stable leader. So, maybe everyone benefits from training the SEAL way.

Get Certified as a Search-and-Rescue Dog

Not all superheroes wear capes. Some just have super-powerful noses, a strong prey drive, and the most selfless human sidekicks ever. Search-and-rescue (SAR) dogs provide a critical service all over the world. Not only do they spring into action to search for missing children, people who are lost in the wilderness, and survivors of natural disasters, but they also provide hope to the distraught families who believe their loved one will be safely located.

For handlers, search and rescue is volunteer work. "It's a passion," says Pam Medhurst, who has been working in search and rescue for twenty-two years, primarily with beagles. "A lot of people I know who do this work will do it until they physically can't anymore." It's the gratitude that keeps drawing her back. "The families of the missing are always so grateful to have people helping. Any

Danie

time the call goes out, and it's raining or hot or the middle of the night and I don't want to go, I think of the families, and I do it for them."

Dogs, on the other hand, aren't quite as selfless. SAR dogs have been trained to associate the smell of the person they are looking for with their most favorite reward—food or playtime with their favorite toy. So, while it might *seem* like Snickers is sniffing out of love for mankind, he is mainly thinking about his ball. Search-and-rescue dogs *really* want their ball. They want their ball so badly that they will do absolutely anything to find the smell associated with it: traverse treacherous terrain, march through blizzards, walk across unstable buildings, and even climb ladders. No matter how hard the search gets, a great SAR dog believes that what they are looking for is out there if they just keep sniffing.

The human member of the SAR team is usually the more difficult creature to train. "We're the stupid end of the leash," Medhurst admits. She explains that in searches, it can be hard to trust the dog's nose. "You're out there and the dog wants to go one way, and you think the person couldn't have possibly gone that way, and so you pull the dog a different way." More often than not, the dog is right. "You've got to put a lot of trust in the dog. Let go and know that the dog will do what you trained it to do."

Most humans and canines do not have the time, determination, and skill set to become a SAR team. Dogs must train for nearly two years, and humans often train for longer. Medhurst has seen all types of purebreds and mutts grow into successful SAR dogs, but beagles, bloodhounds, and Labrador retrievers are a few of the most common candidates. Medhurst lives with her five beagles—Snickers, Charley, Wishbone, Huckleberry, and Danie, a sprightly nineteen-year-old pooch.

FIND IT!

Most SAR dogs start training when they are puppies. If your canine's puppyhood has passed, you can still play stimulating "find it" games at home. One game SAR puppies-in-training play is hide-and-seek. One human hides while another asks, "Where's Fern? Where's Fern?" (This is also a great way to teach your dog your name.) When the dog looks around the house and finds the person who is hiding, reward him with treats and praise. He may not become a search-and-rescue hero, but he's still a good boy.

3
Travel & Adventure
Did You Say . . . Car Ride?

One of the hardest things about being a dog mom is that moment right before I leave the house to go on vacation. I grab my keys and my wallet, wheel my luggage to the door, then look down at my pooch, who seems to be under the impression she is coming, too. On a humans-only vacation, I'm forced to give my pup a few gentle pets, apologize, and part ways. But on a *dog*-friendly vacay, I grab the leash, she jumps with joy, and we stampede down the stairs . . . together!

Your next dog adventure could be your best trip yet! Just prepare yourself for a car full of dog hair, slobber, the occasional terrible smell, and a whole world full of new experiences.

BACK ROW: April, P.J., Diego, Belle
FRONT ROW: Lilo, Stitch, Merida, Violet, Jazz

Hike to the Top of the Highest (Dog-Friendly) Mountain

With help from Chester, Gretel, and Jessica Williams, blogger, influencer, and Dachshund enthusiast, @youdidwhatwithyourweiner

Think your pup has what it takes to become the top dog? Like, the tip-top dog? At an elevation of 14,433 feet and located in the Rocky Mountains of Colorado, Mount Elbert is the highest dog-friendly mountain in the United States (and the second highest *mountain* in the Lower 48). Jessica Williams, an avid outdoorswoman and blogger, and her two ten-inch-tall miniature wieners have climbed to the top of Mount Elbert. Whoever said small dogs can't hike has never met Chester and Gretel and their amazing human.

Williams believes that small dogs everywhere (especially Dachshunds) should be exploring places way beyond your lap. "In my experience, many people choose to get small dogs because they think they don't need much exercise. The thing is that the size of the dog doesn't equate to the amount of exercise they need. Some small dog breeds, like Dachshunds, actually have significant exercise requirements."

Summiting Mount Elbert was no walk in the park. Of the two main routes to the summit, Williams recommends the South Mount Elbert Trail for hikers with dogs. The trail begins at 9,560 feet, gains 4,850 feet of elevation, and is 11.6 miles round trip. Reaching the summit can take between seven and ten hours. Although hiking this trail doesn't require any special technical preparation (there are no ropes, oxygen tanks, or crampons), you should be physically fit in general. To train for long, high-elevation hikes with your dog, Williams recommends starting out on flatter trails of around three miles. Once you can do that regularly, start increasing the length and elevation of the trail to work up to your goals.

"No, I don't have to carry them."
– Jessica Williams

If the top of Mount Elbert seems too far away, that is completely understandable! Here are a few other canine-approved walks with amazing views, and a little less vertical.

🐾 DOG MOUNTAIN,
SKAMANIA COUNTY, WASHINGTON
Distance: 6.9 miles
Elevation: 2,800 feet

🐾 THE OWLS HEAD,
FRANKLIN COUNTY, NEW YORK
Distance: 1.2 miles
Elevation: 460 feet

🐾 CATHEDRAL ROCK,
SEDONA, ARIZONA
Distance: 1.2 miles
Elevation: 744 feet

🐾 ALABAMA HILLS,
LONE PINE, CALIFORNIA
Multiple hikes and walks in this area.

🐾 MANDEVILLE CANYON
LOS ANGELES, CALIFORNIA
Distance: 7.1 miles
Elevation: 1,102 feet

LEFT: Xena, Cathedral Rock

RIGHT: Chewie, Alabama Hills

Order Room Service at a Fancy Hotel

WITH HELP FROM COURTNEY DASHER AND TUNA,
@TUNAMELTSMYHEART AND @THETRAVELINGTUNA

From doggy swim classes to massage treatments and award-winning room service, some hotels are offering canine amenities beyond the complimentary bone at check-in. When it comes to splurging on a fancy getaway with your VIP (Very Important Pup), how do you pick the perfect destination? The Traveling Tuna has got you covered!

Tuna is a nine-year-old Chiweenie and Instagram sensation with an impressive two million followers and the cutest overbite ever. He's also a trusted face of luxury canine travel. The jet-setting Tuna has been to multiple countries and numerous states sniffing out hotels that take the comfort of pets as seriously as the comfort of their human guests. His travel companion, Courtney Dasher, reviews their favorite experiences at thetravelingtuna.com, focusing primarily on accommodations in the United States and the United Kingdom.

So, what are you waiting for? Nap in Egyptian cotton sheets! Watch squirrels from floor-to-ceiling windows! Indulge in a sweet life of poolside pampering, room service, and gourmet treats! Just, uh, don't expect your pooch to slowly savor each bite of that aged porterhouse steak.

SOME OF TUNA'S FAVORITE PLACES TO STAY

🐾 ARTIST RESIDENCE,
PENZANCE, UNITED KINGDOM

Dine at the charming Cornish Barn smokehouse, walk around the historic seaside town, play on one of the many picture-perfect beaches, and snuggle by the fire at this lovely Georgian inn. *Ah, isn't this lovely!*

🐾 THE CARY ARMS & SPA,
DEVON, UNITED KINGDOM
Go for a walk along Devon's famous coastline, and let your best bud sniff secluded coves and jump in the waves at a wealth of dog-friendly beaches around Torbay.

🐾 NOELLE,
NASHVILLE, TENNESSEE
Located downtown in Nashville's historic Broadway District, Noelle adores dogs of all shapes and sizes. Tuna fancies smelling the streets on Broadway and going for a walk along the Cumberland River.

🐾 THE RITZ CARLTON,
DORADO BEACH, PUERTO RICO
Dogs (thirty pounds and under) can go for a kayak ride, play fetch on white sandy beaches, swim with their human in a private plunge pool, or even take a relaxing bike ride using specialized dog-friendly bikes. Canines are also spoiled with customized tepee-style beds, homemade dog food from award-winning chefs, and, of course, in-room massages. I mean, bow. Wow. *Wow.*

"Tuna has taught me how to be intentional about making others feel seen, known, loved, and adored. Traveling with him has allowed me to meet so many people that I may not have otherwise had the opportunity to meet if he wasn't in my life. The testimonies of people who have written to me telling me of the difference Tuna makes in their days has had a profound effect on me and thus propelled me to pay attention to others more intentionally."–Courtney Dasher

Visit the Dog Chapel

No dogmas allowed, but all dogs are welcome! Dog Mountain is 150 acres of mountaintop paradise in St. Johnsbury, Vermont. Created by author and artist Stephen Huneck (1948–2010) and his wife, Gwen Huneck (1951–2013), Dog Mountain offers endless trails for running, ponds for swimming, and agility courses. "I wanted people and dogs to have the most fun they possibly could," wrote Huneck in 2010. There's snowshoeing in winter, wildflowers in summer, and the most impressive dog parties ever, but what's most moving about this place is the Dog Chapel. "Since dogs are family members, too," Huneck wrote, "I thought it would be wonderful if we could create a spiritual space to help achieve closure and lessen the pain when we lose a beloved dog." Carved completely by hand, the Dog Chapel looks like a classic white New England country church. People of any belief system are welcomed through its doors to honor their departed canine family member. "I had envisioned maybe someday having the foyer filled top to bottom with dog pictures. I never anticipated the whole building—every single space—covered with photos and words of remembrance, as the chapel is today," wrote Huneck. "It is a very moving experience—sad, certainly, but also uplifting—to see how much everyone cherishes his or her dog." Visit the Dog Chapel with your dog and say a prayer of gratitude for your most loyal best friend.

Pip

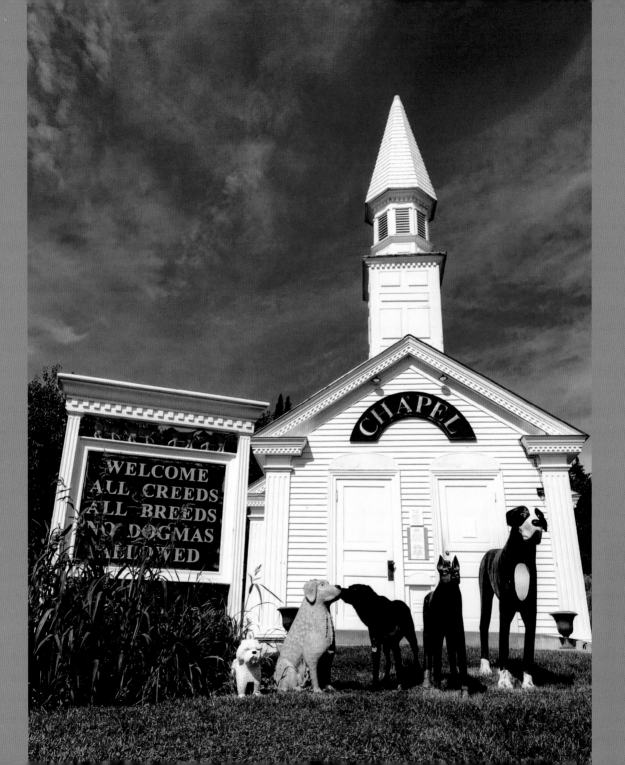

Go Biscuit Tasting

WITH HELP FROM FRENCHIE, @FRENCHIE_WINERY AND CRAIG MCGILL AND SUSAN ELLIOTT, AUTHORS OF *WINE DOGS*, @WINEDOGS_HQ

Sure "wine tasting" might not sound like the most obvious *dog* adventure, but a walk on a vineyard followed by a comfortable air-conditioned tasting room is enjoyable for both two and four-legged creatures.

Your first dog-friendly wine destination must be Frenchie Vineyards in Napa Valley. The *pup*rietor of this vineyard is, of course, Frenchie the French bulldog, a very humble leader who believes all creatures should enjoy the beauty of a great tasting room. Under his leadership, the tasting room is open to the four-legged public. A steady stream of biscuits is readily available. So, while you're admiring the pretty purple of the pinot or sniffing for cedar in the Sangiovese, you can take comfort in knowing your dog is *certainly* doing the same with the different bone varieties. *Ah, I am getting notes of—sniff, sniff—bacon? Is that a . . . CHOMP! Refill, please?*

Whether you're in the wine country of California or another incredible wine destination, remember that your pup will also enjoy sharing the day tasting full-bodied biscuits and tantalizing treats. For a definitive guide to dog-loving wineries around the globe, check out winedogs.com. *Ah, yes, this biscuit pairs well with a nice belly rub!*

Frenchie of Frenchie Vineyards in Saint Helena, California

Take a Herding Vacation

Does your dog ever nip your heels unexpectedly? He's not trying to hurt you. He wants to herd you. Herding dogs inherit a natural instinct to move animals around. So, if you don't bring your pooch to a farm to work, he may try working from home. With you.

"So many people come here and are like, 'My dog herds the kids! My dog herds the cat! My dog herds all the dogs at the dog park!'" explains Nola Jones, champion herding trainer, livestock judge, and owner of Performance Dogs in Action, a herding and agility school in Pleasant Grove, California. "But until a dog herds *livestock,* he hasn't herded." Herding is one of the oldest canine professions. Instead of trying to train the hardwired instinct out of your dog, why not help your pooch learn how to use his special skill?

Of course, just because your dog circles the Roomba in what appears to be a strategic fashion, that does not guarantee he will be any good at making the sheep go through the gate. "The first thing we do is evaluate the dog's sustained interest," explains Jones. A good herding dog sees sheep for the first time and it's nearly impossible to snap the dog's attention away. It's like trying to pry a twelve-year-old away from a video game—sometimes it takes two people! Dogs also need to know that chasing the sheep is not the same as herding the sheep. Making the livestock move in the direction the human wants them to go is herding the sheep. Dogs and humans work together to herd, using the positions on a clockface as reference points. If the human stands at six and the sheep are in the center of the field (the center of the clockface), the dog must know to go to twelve to move the sheep back to the human. This is called "gathering," and it's not so different from running out to fetch the ball, except, like, the ball goes *bahhhh!* The ball moves when you approach it. There's more than one ball. And the balls are *sheep*! FUN!

Kaj

82

RIGHT: Jolene

LEFT: Lynn

Jones told me that beginner dogs are often just excited to be out on a field making the sheep move, so it's OK if they aren't collie material. She's trained all types of dogs how to herd. Herders learn an extensive vocabulary, and people who own herding dogs always give them one-syllable names so it's easier to catch their attention and communicate. *Come by, Grit! Away to me, Luke! Walk up, Scout!* But Jones says the best herding dogs are the older ones—the ones who have been around the farm a few times. You don't have to say anything to them. "You open the gate, he runs in there and does what he's supposed to do perfectly, then looks at you, like, OK close the gate. We're done here."

That'll do, dog. That'll do.

Go Truffle Hunting

When the news broke that a dog in Italy had found a $300,000 truffle, I couldn't help but think—wow, that's why truffle fries are so expensive and could Bette possibly learn to sniff for truffles?

A truffle is a rare and edible fungus that grows underground near the trunks of trees. The funky, sought-after delicacy is a symbol of status and luxury, but you do not have to travel to the Italian countryside to find it. Wild Oregon truffles sell for as much as $200 a pound, and they are buried in the misty forests of the Pacific Northwest like lusty little treasures! There is just one requirement when it comes to finding them: a dog. Well, at least I've got that part covered.

To further explore the Bette-Fernie truffle-business venture, I set off to Eugene, Oregon, for the annual Oregon Truffle Festival, which is a four-day extravaganza with truffles and dogs everywhere. There's a school that trains dogs to hunt for truffles, a one-of-a-kind truffle competition for

dogs called the Joriad, truffle-hunting excursions, and delectable truffles being shaved across your plate at every meal. Coincidentally, lots of canines even had the name, you guessed it, Truffles! Interested in your own truffle start-up? Here's what I learned in truffle school.

STEP 1: SCENT PAIRING

The first step to becoming a truffle-hunting dog is pairing the truffle scent with your dog's favorite treat. Your dog needs to learn: *When I smell this (truffle), I get this (treat).* Dip a cotton swab in truffle oil, and place it inside a small plastic container with air holes. Hold the container down by your side for the dog to sniff. *Smell the truffle? Get a treat!* Repeat.

STEP 2: HIDE THE SCENT

Once your dog associates the valuable truffle scent with a reward, hide the scent. Start with easy spots: behind the leg of a chair, under a table, next to the bed. Walk

Nettle looking
for truffles

your dog around the house on a leash, and the moment she sniffs the truffle, give her a reward. Keep the training sessions short (five to ten minutes) and always end on a positive note.

STEP 3: ENTHUSIASM

Truffle hunting is a team activity where humans and canines are in constant communication, and sometimes humans are tougher to train than dogs. "Enthusiasm is crucial," explains Dr. Charles Lefevre, pioneer of the North American truffle industry and human to two Lagotto Romagnolos, named Dante and Mocha. "If you are not embarrassed in front of your neighbors while you're training your dog to find truffles, you are not being enthusiastic enough."

STEP 4: THE HUNT

Black and white truffles are found in the Pacific Northwest. On the second day of truffle-hunting school, canine students and their eager humans set off on their first forest hunt. All twenty-seven dogs found at least one truffle, and some canines found over twenty! As it turns out, any dog really can learn to sniff for truffles. That is, if you know where to look.

COMPETE IN THE JORIAD

The Joriad is North America's only truffle-hunting competition for dogs, and once a year, canines of all ages and breeds gather in Eugene, Oregon, to compete. The competition is all about encouraging new dogs to hunt for truffles, so contestants must be amateurs (meaning Dante and Mocha can't participate).

In the first two rounds, dogs are tested on their ability to search out truffle oil–scented targets hidden in bins across an arena. When the dog detects the musty aroma, the handler uses a rake or towel to dig in the dirt and find it. Once the human discovers the vial containing the scent, the judge rushes over and confirms the find by holding up a hand and shouting, "truffle!" The crowd goes wild! The dog gets a treat! The top five noses advance to the final round, held in a secret forest location, where dog-and-human teams have an hour to search for as many truffles as they can find. The dog who finds the most is crowned truffle champion. But the humans are the real winners here. Thanks to dogs, we get to eat truffles.

THE LAGOTTO ROMA-WHAT-LO?

The Lagotto Romagnolo (la-goh-toe roman-yolo) is the most prized truffle-hunting dog breed. A curly-haired, fun-loving, water retriever from Northern Italy, this is the only dog in the world bred specifically for truffle hunting. To train your dog the "Lagotto" way, consider speaking in Italian:

Lavoro = Work!

Dov'è (dough-vay) = Where is it?

Trovolo = Find it!

Tartufo = Truffle !

Trova il tartufo = Find the truffle!

Bravo cane (ca-nay) = Good doggy!

ABOVE: The Joriad

LEFT: Bruno, the Lagotto Romagnolo

Stay in a Beagle-Shaped Hotel

Welcome to the Dog Bark Park Inn, the world's biggest beagle! Standing high along Highway 95 in Cottonwood, Idaho, this beagle-shaped bed-and-breakfast is the stay of a lifetime. Despite what you might guess from the appearance of this place, the hotel does accept human guests. Known as "Sweet Willy," this special piece of "barkitecture" features one dog-themed guest room where you and your pooch can snuggle inside the giant head of the beagle. (which is probably not something you ever thought you'd say). "We think nearly everyone identifies with a beagle. It's a breed of dog that has been in America from nearly its earliest days," says Frances Conklin, who built the property with her husband, chainsaw artist Dennis Sullivan. "Have we owned one? No,

although we love them, it is the wrong breed of dog for us. Our favorite breed to own is the golden retriever, of which Sprocket is our current furry ambassador."

Equipped with everything dogs (and their admirers) could desire, the pooch palace is the only dog-shaped building in the world where people and their pups can spend the night. Canine guests can dine on delectable dog biscuits while humans enjoy freshly baked dog-shaped cookies. Animals can relax in the big comfy bed or go for a walk on the wide-open, freshly cut Idaho grass. The Dog Bark Park Inn opened its doors in 1997 and has been a doggy-tourism destination ever since. Book a weekend stay in Idaho or make this a must-see stop on a road trip across the country.

Dig without Getting into Trouble

ABOVE: Deano, the Earthdog

LEFT: Izzy

Originally bred to hunt underground and help farmers control moles, rats, and other vermin, terriers and Dachshunds aren't acting out when they dig up your entire bed of azaleas, they are only trying to help.

If you've got a small, passionate digger, consider signing up for an AKC Earthdog test. Earthdog tests are noncompetitive events held around the country that test a dog's ability to dig and hunt underground. Caged (and unharmed) quarry are hidden within pitch-black tunnels, and the dogs must bravely follow their noses to find them. The tiny terriers navigate mazes, climb over obstacles, and squeeze through dark passageways to descend into the den of a fierce, untamed, wild animal—the rat. Sounds like the worst haunted house ever to me, but the little dogs love it. When the canine finally finds the rat, she yelps and barks with excitement. And for once, the human does not bark back, "No, my flowers!" Instead, the human showers his or her dog with praise and treats. I'd call that a win-win for all. Well, unless you're a rat.

Learn to Howl

With help from Kiba and Linus Zetterlund, @aussiekiba

Is there anything more haunting than the sound of wolves howling into the night? Wolves howl to maintain relationships with their pack, communicate their locations, warn each other about predators, and stay connected. Bette is distantly related to wolves—does she instinctively want to howl? *Can* she howl? If she unleashes her howl will it somehow make her feel connected to her ancestors?

Curious whether my girl could release her inner *a-oooo*, I played YouTube videos for Bette that were "guaranteed to make your dog howl." I amused her with the sounds of ambulance sirens, blew into a harmonica, blasted the calls of Malamutes. Video after video and I got a few ear perks and head tilts, but no howling. Next, I stumbled upon a video on Instagram of an Australian shepherd influencer named Kiba and his human, Linus Zetterlund, sitting on the floor howling *together*. Like a legit pack! How did Zetterlund do it?

"Kiba was quiet as a pup," Zetterlund explains. "But he seems to understand a lot of what I am saying. I like the idea of making some kind of effort of communicating in his language." This made sense. I'd spent years trying to teach Bette my language, but I'd made very little effort to learn hers. Suddenly, I felt like that American who travels abroad and does not even attempt to say hello in the country's language. (I mean, in Nepal, I figured out at least a few key phrases and words. Of course, it helped tremendously that hello and goodbye were both "Namaste"). Maybe I should try to speak Canine? Zetterlund told me his trick to teaching his dog to howl was practicing the howl himself. "Pretend you're talking about your dog's day, put your heart into it, and hopefully you'll get the reaction you want!" In his videos, Linus releases a high-pitched *a-ooooo*, followed by a lower pitch *rarrrr, rarrr, rarrrr* sound. "Even though I have no clue what we're saying,

Kiba

if anything at all, it's nice to have a little 'chat' with your dog."

So, I looked at Bette and gave it a whirl. She cocked her head and started pacing around the room, then rushed to me, jumping and pawing with excitement! *Is my howling working? Are we communicating? Am I sending you important messages?!* Eh, probably not. Bette didn't howl back but

pretending to speak Canine was kind of fun. Plus, it was a nice reminder that I should always be making more effort to understand my distant neighbors. Whether it be through talking, listening, or even taking a road trip to explore a new place (see page 102). Just tell Siri to play Warren Zevon "Werewolves of London." *Aaaaaaooooooooo!*

95

Become a National Park
B.A.R.K. Ranger

WITH HELP FROM AMY BURKERT, WORLD TRAVELER AND FOUNDER OF GOPETFRIENDLY.COM, @GOPETFRIENDLY

From stalagmite-filled caves and sapphire lakes to hot springs and rainforests, the glories of America's national parks system attract millions of tourists a year. Visiting a national park is something everyone should check off their bucket list. Visiting a national park with your *dog*, however, comes with more red tape. National parks are filled with pristine wilderness, unfamiliar environments, and precious wildlife, so it's crucial to be a good human and obey "No Dogs Allowed" signs. This, however, does not mean your canine has to stay in the kennel. Amy Burkert, founder of gopetfriendly.com, traveled in a motorhome for ten years with her husband and their two dogs, a Shar-pei named Ty (2004–2019) and Buster, a German shepherd (2007–2020). The pack traveled more than 100,000 miles together, visited all of the Lower 48 states at least twice, and explored 27 national parks. Although some parks are more dog-friendly than others, Burkert has a few canine-friendly favorites: Acadia National Park in Maine, Grand Canyon National Park in Arizona, and White Sands National Park in New Mexico.

One of the most rewarding parts about traveling to national parks with your dog is becoming a National B.A.R.K. Ranger. At select parks, humans can collect B.A.R.K. Ranger badges and tags for their dogs to wear. OK, so there is no official swearing-in ceremony, sweet uniform, or flat-brimmed hat involved, but ranger duties are not to be taken lightly. B.A.R.K. stands for **Bag your poop**; **Always wear a leash**; **Respect the wildlife**; **Know where you can go**. So, even though you may not be able to bring your canine romping through the hoodoos of Bryce Canyon or on backcountry trails of

Buster and Ty

Yellowstone, you and your dog will fill a more important role by setting a good example for other traveling canines (well, more specifically, their humans) to follow the B.A.R.K, principles and help protect our nation's parks!

Make New Friends

There's something about a dog park that makes it seem as if there might be hope for the world. I open the metal gate, free my dog from her leash, and discover a world where mastiffs are playing with pugs, Chihuahuas are chasing beagles, and humans are socializing with other humans, enjoying the camaraderie of being dog lovers. Ranging from off-leash hours in New York City's Central Park to elaborate fenced-in playgrounds in Florida, the world is full of special places where canines can enjoy an afternoon of butt-sniffing, playing, and chasing (no human attached).

🐾 BERKELEY, CALIFORNIA

Berkeley, California, is home to what many consider the world's first official dog park. Ohlone Dog Park was founded in 1979 and sparked a trend of pet playgrounds across the country.

🐾 PORTLAND, OREGON

With thirty-three public off-leash areas, Portland, Oregon, has the most dog parks per capita of any large US city. Mount Tabor Dog Park is a favorite. With towering trees to protect you and your pooch from the rain, this dog run, although only partially fenced, is a perfect place to train your pup to hike off-leash.

🐾 NEW YORK CITY, NEW YORK

Tompkins Square Dog Run is New York City's first and largest dog park. Before the dog run was opened in 1990, Tompkins Square Park was ridden with crime. Today, even those who don't have dogs credit the canines for bringing the park back to the community. This no-frills, East Village gem is the perfect place to spend a Saturday morning with your pooch. The park also hosts the largest Halloween dog parade in the world!

Moody and Luna

Uptown, New York City's beloved Central Park morphs into a magical canine Utopia during off-leash hours. Before 9 a.m. and after 9 p.m., city dogs can run free in Manhattan's biggest backyard.

🐾 JOHNS CREEK, GEORGIA

With a full agility course, hoops for jumping, and tunnels for scampering, many consider Newtown Dream Dog Park the Six Flags Over Georgia for dogs.

🐾 JACKSONVILLE, FLORIDA

Dog Wood Park is forty-two acres of fitness, relaxation, and fun for canines and their humans. It's more of a "social club" than a dog park, and humans must pay a small fee to enter. Spend the afternoon tossing a Frisbee and running on the trails. Go for a swim in Lake Bow Wow, or check out Lake Fifi, the "small dogs only" swimming pond.

🐾 ADA, MICHIGAN

Shaggy Pines Dog Park costs a few bones to get in, but with agility-training courses, fifteen acres of fenced-in fun, a one-mile jogging trail, and a coffee bar to "sit and stay," this doggy social club is worth the entry fee. There's also a giant sand pile called Doggy Mountain, perfect for canines who love to climb and dig.

🐾 NAMPA, IDAHO

One of the only parks with designated playing areas for small dogs, big dogs, and senior dogs, Nampa Dog Park offers expansive grassy areas for walking, a wading pond for swimming, a dock for jumping, and six acres for sniffing.

🐾 LOS ANGELES, CALIFORNIA

At the top of Mulholland Drive, tucked away in Laurel Canyon, is a magical, three-acre dirt oasis where many of Hollywood's most beautiful people and their equally beautiful pups play. Is that Ryan Gosling and his dog, Lucho?

Moody

Go on a Road Trip

"**It must be like olfactory fireworks** for dogs," explains Alexandra Horowitz, *New York Times* bestselling author and leading researcher in dog cognition, after I ask why dogs love sticking their heads out of car windows. Odors are everywhere. Smells don't just live on fire hydrants and sidewalks and grass. They travel through the air. So, the amount of smells flying past a nose stuck out a car window must be off the charts!

I know car rides are one of *Bette's* favorite things, but having my dog as my co-pilot is one of my favorite things, too. Bette (unlike my ex-boyfriend) never tries to change the radio station in the middle of my favorite T-Swift song. She doesn't bark when I miss the turn or whine "*Are we there yet?*" Plus, she listens to me. Okay, maybe she doesn't *listen* listen to me. Like, that wasn't what I meant when I said we needed to "gas up the car," Bette. (Talk about olfactory experiences!) But, no sweat, girl. We'll just roll down the windows again, crank up those tunes, and keep on cruising. Here we go!

Joyce, Nika, and Neon

TRIP #1: TRAVEL LIKE CHARLEY

Charley was a standard poodle best known for accompanying his human, the great American author, John Steinbeck on a three-month, 10,000-mile road trip around the United States. Charley barked at bears in Yellowstone National Park, stuck his head out the window while cruising the Avenue of the Giants in California, and begged for lobster in Maine. Most importantly, Charley serves as Steinbeck's trusty ambassador through their thirty-eight-state adventure, always ready to help make friends on the road. "A dog is a bond between strangers," writes the author in his bestselling travelogue, *Travels with Charley*. Today, the book serves as a road map for other dogs and humans to "travel like Charley" and set off on epic cross-country road trips.

Floyd

Pip

TRIP #2: GET YOUR LICKS ON ROUTE 66

Offering quirky roadside diners, wild national parks, and iconic landmarks, the famous Route 66 travels from Chicago to Santa Monica. Visit the "Dawgy Corral" at the Big Texan Steak Ranch & Brewery. Stop and see one of the world's largest balls of twine. Mark your territory by spray-painting your pup's name at the eccentric Cadillac Ranch in Amarillo, Texas. Or become a B.A.R.K. Ranger at the Petrified Forest National Park in Arizona.

TRIP #3: DRIVE THE ALASKA HIGHWAY

The 1,390-mile two-lane Alaska Highway stretches from Dawson Creek, British Columbia, to Delta Junction, near Fairbanks, Alaska. Unpaved sections of the highway were common and gas stations were rare. There were no Dairy Queens or fancy hotels, billboards or cell phone signals. But what the journey lacked in amenities, it made up for in breathtaking wilderness. We played fetch in beautiful forests, ate fresh salmon in Haines, and hiked around snow-covered mountains. The only traffic we ever encountered while driving in the Yukon was a herd of bison. And at one point, we watched a grizzly bear cross the road, our noses pressed against the van window in total amazement. We didn't have plush amenities or any other human friends to help us navigate, but we had the open road and each other, and that was enough.

ENJOY A SLOW TRIP

Whether my car ride is a two-month cross-country journey or a two-hour jaunt to hike a new trail, I try not to time our potty breaks like Indy 500 pit stops. We stop and throw the ball, jump in the lake, pull over at scenic vistas I didn't intend to stop. I try to appreciate where I am instead of feeling rushed to arrive somewhere else. It's easy to hurry and need to see it all. Traveling with Bette has taught me that I often see more by intentionally trying to see less, by slowing down and enjoying whatever simple pleasures are around me, like she does.

Bette

PLACES TO FILL UP
ON DOGGY FUEL

☐ STOP FOR POOCHINIS AT SHAKE SHACK

☐ GRAB A PUP PATTY AT IN-N-OUT BURGER

☐ ENJOY A PUPPUCCINO AT STARBUCKS

☐ ORDER A PUPPY LATTE FROM DUNKIN' DONUTS

☐ INDULGE IN PUPCAKES AT SPRINKLE'S CUPCAKES

☐ ASK FOR A "DOG BISCUIT" FROM CHICK-FIL-A

☐ STOP AT TIM HORTONS FOR A SUGAR-FREE
    DOGGY DONUT HOLE

ROCK AND ROLL OVER: A ROAD TRIP PLAYLIST

"I LOVE MY DOG" BY CAT STEVENS

"MARTHA MY DEAR" BY THE BEATLES

"HOUND DOG" BY ELVIS PRESLEY

"OLD KING" BY NEIL YOUNG

"MAN OF THE HOUR" BY NORAH JONES

"GONNA BUY ME A DOG" BY THE MONKEES

"YOU'VE GOT A FRIEND IN ME" BY RANDY NEWMAN

4
Creativity:
Think Outside the Crate

This section is less about dogs flexing their creative muscles and more about humans getting creative with activities they think to do with their dogs. From paw painting to photo shoots to graduating with an Ivy League PawHD, there are tons of opportunities to step out of your daily routine—and comfort zone!—to find new ways to connect with your pup.

Otto

Take Underwater Photos

WITH HELP FROM SETH CASTEEL, AUTHOR OF THE *NEW YORK TIMES* BESTSELLING *UNDERWATER DOGS*

It seems like a simple game: throw a ball in a pool and your dog fetches it (over and over and over again). But have you ever stopped to think about what's going on under the surface? What does your dog look like smashing through the surface of the water for a tennis ball like a shark going after a fish? That's exactly what Seth Casteel, the author and photographer behind *Underwater Dogs* and *Underwater Puppies*, was asking himself when he decided to jump in and find out.

Want to know what *your* dog looks like underwater? You don't need a lot of fancy equipment. Grab a point-and-shoot underwater camera, find a pool, and jump in too!

STEP 1: PLAY FETCH TO WARM UP

"The photographs in *Underwater Dogs* are based on a simple game of fetch, only in the water!" says Casteel. "Once you have established that your dog can successfully play fetch, the next step is adding the water."

STEP 2: FIND A POOL

"Underwater photographs require crystal-clear water, and since the clearest water you will likely find will be in a swimming pool, you will need to help your dog safely get comfortable with the pool, including entering and exiting," explains Casteel. Just because your dog swims in natural bodies of water doesn't mean he or she will jump in a pool right away. Start slow and give your pup an easy way to enter the water, such as a ramp or steps. "I find that most dogs afraid of the pool at first just don't understand it. If your dog can start to explore this new situation a little bit at a time, he will start to gain more and more confidence."

Rhoda

STEP 3: INTRODUCE THE TOY

To get the best photo, you want your dog's head underneath the water, fetching her toy. So, it helps if her toy sinks. "To get the tennis ball to sink, simply cut a small hole in it. You can also use 'squeaker tennis balls' designed for dogs, and when you squeak one underwater, it slowly fills with water, which alters the buoyancy," says Casteel.

STEP 4: BUY, BORROW, OR RENT AN UNDERWATER CAMERA

"I'd suggest a point-and-shoot underwater camera with a strong flash. It's what I used starting out," Casteel recommends. "Expect good-quality pictures, but not professional, at a reasonable price point!"

STEP 5: HOLD YOUR BREATH

"Many people ask if I scuba dive during shoots. If the dogs were scuba diving, I'd be scuba diving, but it has been our collaborative decision to simply hold our breath," jokes Casteel. So, grab a pair of goggles, take a big breath, and have a friend toss the ball in the pool. *Lights! Camera! Splash!*

WHAT BREEDS ARE BEST FOR SWIMMING?

"Most folks expect me to say Labs or golden retrievers are the best water dogs, and sometimes that is true, but I've also seen both of these breeds be timid and have seen Maltese and Chihuahuas go bananas in the pool! You just never know!"

"My favorite thing about dogs is that they are instinctively optimistic creatures, waking each day with a positive outlook on life regardless of the day before." –Seth Casteel

Learn to Paint

WITH HELP FROM DOGVINCI AND YVONNE DAGGER, @DOG_VINCI

His name is Dagger, but his fans call him DogVinci. "The most beautiful part about Dagger is that he has no preconceived knowledge of art history, art genres, and art in general. Wherever the brush lands is where the stroke will be," says the artist's human, Yvonne Dagger, a Long Island professional painter.

"One day, as I was painting at my easel, Dagger approached me and nudged me with his snout. I jokingly asked him if he wanted to paint," she explains. "Dagger's tail wagged immediately. I set up an easel on the floor with a stretched canvas, and I began utilizing the command words he already knew and taught him how to paint." DogVinci was studying to be a service dog as a puppy (he had to drop out because of fear issues), which meant he had already learned the intricate commands that are prerequisites for canine painting (like pushing drawers closed and holding objects in his mouth). "But that really is not enough," warns Yvonne. "A

Dagger, a.k.a. DogVinci

dog must really *want* to paint. Dagger is self-motivated. Dagger loves to paint."

A selfless artist, DogVinci has donated his colorful masterpieces to charity and raised more than $135,000 to help other humans and dogs in need. "Working makes him feel successful," says Yvonne. "Our studio has become a happy place for Dagger, where he can express himself on the canvas." Yvonne reminds me that holding a brush and painting is a simple task for humans, but for dogs it's a complex and extraordinary skill that requires a lot of training. If you think you might have the next Pawcasso on your hands, here are a few steps to give painting with your canine a whirl.

STEP 1: GATHER SUPPLIES

You'll need nontoxic, washable paint (if it's safe for children, it's usually safe for pets, but read labels and ask your veterinarian to be sure); a blank canvas, fabric, or paper; a cardboard paper-towel roll; a one-inch flat paintbrush; duct tape; and scissors. A beret is optional, but encouraged.

STEP 2: MAKE THE BRUSH

Dagger's first brush was made out of a paper towel roll, then he advanced to a wooden dowel. To make the cardboard brush, cut a small hole in the center of a cardboard paper towel roll. Wedge the handle of a paintbrush through the hole, so the two pieces together make the shape of a T, then use duct tape to secure the brush and roll together.

STEP 3: TARGET TRAIN

Use target training to encourage your dog to touch the brush to the canvas. "When I was teaching Dagger how to paint, I used positive affirmation, food rewards, and repetitive command words," says Yvonne. Some command words she uses are "paint," "pick color," and "good."

STEP 4: PAINT

Once your dog is touching the brush to the canvas consistently, start adding paint to the brush. Dagger is trained to touch his nose to select the paint color he wants, but you can also help your dog decide which tones to use.

HAVE A STRUGGLING ARTIST?

Consider paw painting. Any pooch can paw paint. Spread a big piece of paper (fabric or canvas works, too) outside, dip your dog's paws in nontoxic paint, and call her onto the canvas. Invite your dog to express whatever she is feeling. *Sit! Stay! Run! Play! Ah, yes! Call the Metropolitan Museum of Art! It's a masterpiece!*

"Dagger has taught me to never, ever give up. To always use your talents and abilities in the best way you can." –Yvonne Dagger

Dagger's masterpieces from top to bottom:

Botanical Beauty

Here Comes the Sun

Inspirational Bluebird

Stage a Hollywood Photo Shoot

WITH HELP FROM BROOKS MORRISON AND MIKE DEMPSEY,
LOS ANGELES STUNT "PHODOGRAPHERS," @SUPDOGPHOTOGRAPHY

My camera phone is great for snapping selfies with Bette—we've taken plenty of beach, mountain, and "out for a walk in the neighborhood doesn't she look precious" shots together over the years. But I've always wanted a portrait of my dog and me that was more personal than your standard portrait mode shot. I wanted a photo of us that was exciting! Unique! Special! Artistic! One that captured her true emotions and complex personality (but, maybe not *all* of her personality).

That's when I discovered Sup Dog Photography, a cutting-edge pet photography business in LA run by dog-loving photographer Brooks Morrison and Mike Dempsey. With a little Hollywood magic and fancy Photoshop skills, these guys don't just take pictures of pets, they tell stories that celebrate the unique relationships we share with our dogs.

The Sup Dog team began our session with lots of questions about Bette and me and our relationship. I told them about Bette's fears (flies and Chihuahuas), her passions (Road trips! Car rides! Sticks! Squirrels!), and about her lovely overbite and beautiful smile. I also cautioned that sometimes Bette's smile was more of a Joker grin, and that my canine might be a little . . . *difficult on set.* (OK, maybe more than a little.) They reassured me that those characteristics were exactly what they wanted. The ideal spot to capture Bette's beautiful smile and wild spirit was one of our favorite places: the park.

Given Bette's social anxieties, I worried that she might struggle posing for a camera. But thankfully, Morrison and Dempsey assured me that Bette didn't have to pose for the camera. All she had to do was sit in the driver's

Bianca, Patrick, and Gnarly

seat of our parked van and do whatever she wanted to do. "Our human clients can jump onto stunt mats, balance on a ladder, fly off a trampoline, contort their bodies, or do whatever it takes to get the shot," Morrison told me. "Our dog clients, on the other hand, don't give a damn about schedules or props or lights, so they require us to be creatively flexible. We are always on dog time."

As I threw myself onto a stunt mat, over and over again trying to get the shot, Bette didn't do much of anything but stick her head out the window to watch. "Great job, Bette! Who's a good girl? Yes, you are! Yes, you are!" Morrison beamed, tossing her another biscuit. "Fern, can you jump a little higher this time?"

These guys took it to the next level with ladders, props, costume changes, and perfect lighting. Bette was all in on the experience—as long as the biscuits kept coming. However, her "wild side" might have revealed itself when Dempsey cranked up the leaf blower to make my hair blow just right, and of course, to make me feel kind of like Beyoncé. Sure, having a professional photo shoot with my dog was certainly a more human-focused activity, but I don't think Bette minded the steady stream of treats, the car ride, and the bonus trip to the park. The shoot only lasted an hour or so, and a week later, I had exactly what I wanted: a photo that captures the loving, joyous, *totally* trustworthy, one-of-a-kind relationship I share with my dog.

Learn a Dance Move

WITH HELP FROM FALCO AND LUKAS PRATSCHKER, @LUKASANDFALCO

"First, you need good treats." Lukas Pratschker emphasized. "Your dog will never do any good dance moves without good treats." This I completely understood. At weddings, I would not do any of my good dance moves without the "treats" either. So, I grabbed Bette's favorite milkbones, moved the furniture in the living room, threw on a pair of cute sweats, and called my dance partner to the stage. Bette (clearly very excited to be at dance practice) was already burning up the floor with some of her signature moves: the *jump-on-two-legs-and-bite-mom's sleeve* move and (her personal favorite) the *run-around-the-house-as-fast-as-possible-for-15-seconds-with-no-regards-to-humans-or-furniture-or-anything-else-animate-or-inanimate* move. Although she did choreograph these "routines" herself, I was thankful we were about to start training with professionals.

Pratschker and his border collie Falco are a canine freestyle team from Vienna,

"Falco, you were just... *amazing*."
—Simon Cowell

Austria. I first saw the duo on Season 14 of *American's Got Talent*, where they dazzled the stage in some of the most beautiful, tear-worthy, doggy dance spectacles ever. They twirled! They jumped through hoops! They leapt and ran and rolled over! At one point, Falco even drove a Jeep. Most impressively, the duo received a standing ovation from the toughest, most famous judge ever—Simon Cowell! Now, Pratschker has his own doggy dancing school called *School of Dogs*, where he has trained hundreds of dogs—from Yorkshire terriers to great danes—to bust a move with their humans.

Pratschker told me that a great place to start training your doggy dance partner is with the "Leg Weave." In this move, your dog learns to weave between your legs in the shape of a Figure 8. He says that you should try to get your dog to follow your hand, and *then* reward with a treat (instead of teaching your dog to simply follow the treat). At first, Bette was not following my

127

hand at all. I'd put my hand out and try to guide her between my legs, and she'd bite it, paw it, or bark at it. My instinct was to blame my pup for not getting the routine right, but Pratschker reminded me that dog dancing is about clear communication. When the dog doesn't understand what to do, it is the *human* who needs to try clearer signals. So, I practiced my signals, I blasted inspiring Broadway tunes, kept it upbeat, encouraging, and positive and soon we reached leg weave perfection. *Great job, Bette! We will bring Simon Cowell to tears in no time. Let's practice again, girl! Ready, sit!* Bette jumped up and bolted out of the room. Okay, well maybe that *America's Got Talent* thing is a longer-term goal. But, for now, at least we're the stars of *Fern's Living Room's Got Talent.*

PRACTICE WITH HUMANS

"Sometimes when people are training and their dog is doing something wrong, the people tell me their dog is stupid or something like that," Pratschker admitted. When this happens, he recommends that the human try teaching the trick to another *human,* but without using any words. Not only does this help us see how smart our dogs actually are for learning so much without speaking to us, it will also help refine your non-verbal communication skills. The moment your cue becomes unclear and your human friend is confused, he or she can alert you and tell you specifically what motion you need to improve.

"Falco taught me that the most important thing is to enjoy life. I recognize that unfortunately a dog just has a few years on earth, but for me that's also something special. Every time I go outside with him or play with him or train with him, I recognize that. You really have to enjoy every second with your dog." -Lukas Pratschker

Graduate from the Ivy League

Bring your furry child to New Haven and qualify for a very special bumper sticker: "My dog made it to the Ivy League!" The Canine Cognition Center at Yale is a research facility where doggy scholars earn PawHDs by playing problem-solving games with an expert team of scientists. If you are concerned that your pooch may not be smart enough for Yale, don't worry. Your dog does not need a perfect SIT score to get in; the only prerequisite for admission is to be friendly with humans.

At doggy Yale, scientists are devoted to learning more about how canines perceive their environment, solve problems, and make decisions. "The question should not be 'how smart is my dog?'" says Zachary Silver, one of the scientists at the lab. "The question should really be 'in what ways is my dog smart?'" Different animals display intelligence in different ways. What makes *dog* cognition unique is that canines evolved with humans. "Throughout their life spans, dogs have been bombarded with information about human social interactions and social cues. They have put those together to develop a rich understanding of human behavior that is unlike any other animal." One way to learn more about your dog's intelligence is to examine how well she picks up your social cues. Yale's canine scientists test this with a classic hide-the-food-in-a-cup game. All you need is two cups, some treats, and a friend to stage your own Ivy League caliber experiment.

STEP 1: HIDE THE TREAT

Hide a treat underneath one of two identical cups or containers. Make sure your dog doesn't see where you are hiding it. Next, reveal the cups to your dog and point to the one that has the food in

Nutmeg

it. Does your dog follow your point? It might seem like a simple task, but it's not. Pointing is considered to be very human. Not even our closest genetic relatives (chimps and bonobos) can follow the human point. Dogs are the only species that are as good as human children when it comes to understanding this cooperative communication cue.

STEP 2: POINT WITH YOUR HEAD

If your dog passes the finger point, hide the treat again, but this time point with your head. Turn your head forty-five degrees to stare at the cup with the treat. Does your dog follow your gaze? If so, great work! Exemplary performance!

STEP 3: ADD FRIENDS

For the honors level of this game, invite two friends to play. Hide the treat again and have one human watch where you hide it and the other turn around and not watch. Next, reveal the cups to the dog and have the human who knows where the treat is point to the correct cup and the other human point to the incorrect cup. In some contexts, dogs can track who knows where the treat is hidden.

"Playing these types of brain games is a really fun experience for humans and dogs," says Silver. "The more questions we answer, the more new ones we discover." Yale's Canine Cognition Center is always looking for more dog students to enroll, and no need to stress about performance, the graduation rate is exceptionally high.

LEFT: Duncan

RIGHT: Gerda

Set a Guinness World Record

WITH HELP FROM FINLEY AND ERIN MOLLOY, @FINNYBOYMOLLOY

Can your dog hold more than six tennis balls in her mouth at one time? Bark louder than a jackhammer? Jump higher than 6.2 feet? Or pop one hundred balloons in fewer than 28.22 seconds? What about your pup's tongue—is it longer than 7.3 inches? If the answer is yes, you might have a Guinness World Record on your hands.

"Your dog does not have to be a star athlete to attempt a Guinness World Records title. Any human-dog team can attempt a world record. We receive a wide variety of applications," says Christina Fernandez, records manager at Guinness World Records. "Most naturally evolve from people playing with their dogs and noticing something they believe is unique or interesting. From there, owners will often work with their pets to refine that skill and prepare to attempt a Guinness World Records title." That's how it happened with Finley, a six-year-old golden retriever, who holds a Guinness World Record for most tennis balls held in the mouth by a dog. "One afternoon, I was sitting in the backyard, and he came up to me with four tennis balls in his mouth! It gradually increased to six. He's been a ball hoarder for quite some time now," says Erin Molloy, Finley's human. Finley has finally been recognized for this phenomenal talent, but snagging the Guinness World Record wasn't easy. "He had to pick up *all* six tennis balls on his own, have them in his mouth for three seconds, then drop them so they were visible. And we had to have photo evidence, video evidence, and witnesses," says Molloy. It took them over a year to finally earn the title, but Finley seemed to enjoy the process. Great job, Finley!

Do you and your dog have a super-special skill or trick? The folks at Guinness World Records are always on the lookout for new applications from dog owners with amazing pets!

Finley

Official Guinness
WORLD Record Holder

RECORD-BREAKING IDEAS

🐾 MOST CONSECUTIVE TREATS CAUGHT IN A ROW: HAGRID, A GIANT LEONBERGER, HOLDS THE RECORD; HE CAUGHT NINE MINI SAUSAGES IN A ROW. CAN YOUR DOG CATCH TEN?

🐾 MOST DOGS TO EVER HOLD THE SIT-AND-STAY SIMULTANEOUSLY FOR ONE MINUTE: NO ONE HAS SET THIS RECORD. GRAB SOME FRIENDS AND GIVE IT A GO!

🐾 MOST TRICKS PERFORMED IN ONE MINUTE: IN JUST 60 SECONDS, HERO, A BORDER COLLIE, OBEDIENTLY PERFORMED 49 TRICKS. CAN YOU AND YOUR CANINE PERFORM 50?

🐾 LONGEST FLYING-DISC THROW CAUGHT BY A DOG: DAVY, A WHIPPET, CAUGHT A FRISBEE THROW OF 402 FEET.

Become an Influencer

WITH HELP FROM LONI EDWARDS, FOUNDER OF THE DOG AGENCY
AND MOM TO ONE OF THE WORLD'S FIRST CANINE INFLUENCERS, @CHLOETHEMINIFRENCHIE

There's a special time in every owner's life when he or she thinks, "Should my dog have a social media account?" I was that person (OK, so maybe I still am a little bit of that person). Social media is full of adorable canine influencers cashing in on free kibble through modeling gigs and sponsored posts. How hard could it be? I had visions of Bette collar collaborations! Treat and toy endorsements! And all of the new and exciting sponsored vacations we'd get to take together to create content. Bette would love it! Maybe we'd even retire early?

"It is truly the best job," says Loni Edwards, agent to the canine social media stars. She has represented more than 150 of the top animal influencers and founded the first (and, like, only) talent management agency to focus on pets. "You get to spend more time with your furry best friend, you spread joy around the world via your content, you build a whole new community of like-minded dog lovers, you get to work with brands you admire, and you get paid to do it!"

The first step to online fame is making sure your dog is photogenic (Chloe obviously had that one covered). Next, build your dog brand. Think about the mission of your account. Do you want Oscar to raise awareness about adopting senior pets? Perhaps your Yorkie has an empowering rescue story to share? Maybe Francy is the next big foodie? Does your dog have defining characteristics you can play up—an overbite, exceptionally long ears, a tongue that doesn't quite fit in her mouth? "Whatever you do, always stay on brand so your fans know what to expect from you. The more creative the brand, the better you'll stand out," Edwards emphasizes. I stared at Bette's profile, trying to

Chloe enjoying the influencer life

figure out how I would differentiate her from the masses. *Bette. Cat poop connoisseur.* Ugh, too gross. *Bette dearest, bestest, most well-behaved doggy ever.* Well, I don't want to lie. *Bette. Total work in progress. Overbite dog. Lover of squirrels and sticks.* Perfect. She will be an overnight sensation!

Next, we started posting. I posted Bette for a few days in a row at all the strategic times. I tried to be consistent and craft clever captions and engage with other dog owners on Instagram. After a few days, Bette gained around a hundred followers and got some likes, but after a couple of weeks, we were far from finding fame. I felt disappointed. Should I buy Bette followers? Pay for likes? I was certain my dog had what it took to be an influencer. The distinct look. The overbite. The goofy personality. I knew she'd sit

in front of a camera all day, cocking her head in adorable directions and modeling outfits that tested her patience. It was me who lacked motivation. It turns out that doggy Instagram stardom is competitive and a lot of work for humans. I looked at Bette and broke the news that she might not ever have as many followers as Chloe or *need* to sign with Loni as an agent. But . . . could we still just have fun going on adventures and posting cute photos and videos because we want to? Was that okay?

Bette wasn't listening; she was staring out the window waiting for the squirrel (clearly more concerned with the natural world than the social media world). She did look pretty cute sitting there, though. I snapped a photo and posted it. Twelve likes! Great work, girl!

Chloe

MEET MAYOR MAX,
THE FRIENDLIEST
POLITICIAN AROUND

TourIdyllwild.com

IDYLLWILD

LAMAR

most difficult times," says Mueller. "When you think about dogs and the things they can do to help people, that's something they can do. They can comfort people."

Of course, not all canines can be sworn into office, but more can help their communities. "If you have a friendly dog who loves people, I would just take them downtown and let people pet them!" recommends Mueller. "You could even make an agenda and have a purpose. Use your dog to start representing a bigger cause."

Mayor Max's message is unconditional love for everyone, but he's also working towards peace on Earth in his lifetime. Mueller feels that so many humans go through life thinking that bad things happen, and they can't make a difference, but she believes peace on Earth resides within the small actions of every single individual, including dogs. Each of us has an important role to play in making the world a more positive place. Well, I'm just going to put my hands up and say it. Mayor Max for President!

5
Love & Self-Care
Sit, Stay, and *Heal*

Dogs herd and hunt and sniff for us. They see for the blind and search for the missing. In turn, we bathe them, feed them, provide shelter, and scratch behind their ears. But the special relationship we share with our dogs is much more than just a transactional one. Dogs and humans adore each other. We take care of each other. We even *love* each other! It's impossible to know where we would be without canines, and where canines would be about us. Whether you do a DNA test to better understand your four-legged friend, schedule a trip to the groomer, or spend a Friday night on the couch indulging in a special steak dinner together, caring for your dog is a great way to say "I love you, too."

Milly

Have a Date Night

WITH HELP FROM XEPHOS AND CLIVE WYNNE, CANINE SCIENTIST AND AUTHOR OF *DOG IS LOVE*

When I asked Clive Wynne, a pioneering canine behaviorist, what adventure he thought his black mutt, Xephos, might want most in the world, he wasn't sure he wanted to tell me. He thought, maybe it wasn't exciting enough. *Well, what is it?* I pried.

Wynne has conducted cutting-edge research on dogs and their wild relatives. He is the founding director of the Canine Science Collaboratory at Arizona State University. He is the author of several animal cognition books and more than a hundred peer-reviewed scientific journal articles that are some of the most highly cited studies on dog psychology! He's even worked with wolves! There was no way this could be boring.

"Well, we would sit on the couch," he explained to me. I waited for him to continue. He didn't. That was pretty much it.

He would sit on the couch with his dog and give her a nice pet.

"It's what my dog really likes to do!" he exclaimed.

At first, I wanted to reject the notion that sitting on the sofa was a noteworthy adventure. We've got to get up from the couch, people! Move! Run! Play! Sniff! Fetch! But the more Wynne explained, the more I started to understand that this adventure was about more than embracing your inner couch potato.

Wynne told me that what matters to dogs are relationships. Dogs thrive when they are able to forge strong emotional connections. Sure, we love our dogs. But have you ever thought about how incredible it is that the feeling is mutual? I mean, we are two different species!

By researching dogs' hormones, brains, and even heartbeats, Wynne has proven that you are much more than just

Clive and Xephos

a walking treat dispenser to your dog. There is a reason that Bette wants to be next to me or sitting on top of me and looks heartbroken every time she ends up on the wrong side of the door. She *is* heartbroken. According to Wynne, our dogs experience love in a similar way that humans do. Being left alone is one of the saddest things that can happen to a canine.

I thought about the many Friday nights Bette had spent alone while I was out looking for human love, and a pang of guilt fell over me. I decided it was time to step up my game. I brought her a beautiful bouquet of fresh sticks, a nice bottle of water, and some hot dogs (she's a cheap date). Next, I threw on a movie and snuggled on the couch with my girl. Sure, Bette was snoring before the previews were over. And the scents coming from her were no Le Labo. But for once, I didn't have to worry about saying the wrong thing or shoveling too much food in my mouth or spilling on my shirt. I didn't have to stress about being too clingy or wonder whether my date loved me as much as I loved her. All I had to do was relax on the couch and feel relieved that the only game this animal was capable of playing was fetch. Bette snuggled her head in my lap and my heart filled with joy. I had another animal that really *did* love me back. She loved me exactly as I was. Sitting right here on the couch next to her.

Have a Spa Day

WITH HELP FROM JESS RONA, AUTHOR, COMEDIAN, TV HOST, AND GROOMER TO THE STARS, @JESSRONAGROOMING

Most pups hate the B-word, but Instafamous and totally fabulous groomer Jess Rona knows if a B-A-T-H is given with patience and praise, even the most nervous canines will sit and soak up the suds. "The way I handle the dog communicates to them that they are seen, and valued, and I am grateful to them," she says. For Rona, grooming is not only an essential part of caring for your dog's eyes, ears, nails, teeth, and coat; it also helps dogs feel their best and bond with the humans around them. "When dogs feel conditioned and all brushed out, I think they feel better. I know they definitely love the extra attention and snuggles they get from their owners."

Rona has worked in the grooming industry for more than twenty years and has worked with some of the coolest dogs in Hollywood, including Katy Perry's dog, Nugget; the late Marnie, an Instafamous beauty; and even Zooey Deschanel's dogs! At her Los Angeles salon, canine customers are spoiled with blowouts, blueberry facials, and, of course, lots of love and treats.

If you're giving your pup a bath or trim at home, Rona recommends getting a pair of thinning sheers. "They're much more forgiving than a regular pair of sheers." Also, condition your canine's coat, brush regularly, and try not to treat bathing your dog like it's another chore you don't have time to do. "Dogs are energy readers," reminds Rona. "They don't live in the past. They are right there in the present with you." If we're rushed and stressed, *they* are stressed. So, throw on some happy music, grab the soap, and enjoy an afternoon caring for your special friend.

Try a Doga Pose

Yoga is an ancient discipline that unifies the mind, breath, and body. Doga *is* yoga, but, like, with your dog. "Dogs pick up on our energy. When we are calm, our dogs are calm," says Portland doga instructor Pam Blair. Blair emphasized how humans practice yoga to unify the mind and body and find the present moment. Dogs appear to have already achieved the whole "finding the present moment" thing, so they are a natural match for yoga, obviously.

The beauty of doga (and yoga) is that you do not need fancy leggings, a flexible physique, or an expensive studio membership to do it. You and your dog already have everything you need to practice, exactly as you are! So, roll out your mat or plop right down on that pile of clothes. One straightforward pose that's great for beginners is a seated twist. In doga, Blair calls this position the "Heart to Heart."

SIT

To begin your practice, bring yourself to a cross-legged seated position on the floor and ask your dog to sit next to you, on your right side.

NAMASTAY

Greet your dog with "namaste," then kindly ask your canine to nama*stay*.

BREATHE AND PET

Next, close your eyes and take a few slow breaths, in through your nose and out through your mouth. With your eyes still closed, give your dog some soft, gentle pets, making small circles with your hands across his or her fur. Do this for a minute or two and continue to breathe.

Note: If your dog would rather practice "downward-facing human" on the couch or fill the room with the powerful and healing sounds of their squeaky toy—that's okay. Doga is about living in harmony with all beings exactly as they are in the present moment. Just keep breathing.

STRETCH

After a minute or two, lift both hands up towards the sky as you breathe in, stretching your fingertips up to the birds and trees and squirrels.

HUG

When you're ready, bring your arms down, release your breath, and twist your chest to the right side to meet your dog for a hug. Ideally, you'd be "heart to heart" with your dog. (But again, doga is all about acceptance.) Take another breath as you hug your dog, then release your hands. For a balanced practice, do the twist again on your left side. Good, dogis!

Bilbo, a German shepherd-Shar-Pei mix, in the downward dog

Get a Massage

WITH HELP FROM GENE RUKAVINA, CERTIFIED CANINE MASSAGE THERAPIST

Take your dog to a certified canine massage therapist (yes, that's a thing) and treat them to a rejuvenating experience way beyond the mere belly scratch. Canine masseuses can be found around the country and can help relieve tension and pain in our beloved pets. Alternatively, you could turn on peaceful music, make a comfortable bed on the floor, and invite your canine to embrace the tranquility, healing, and bliss of the massage at home. "There is no wrong way to massage a dog, as long as you aren't rubbing bones directly," says Gene Rukavina, a canine masseuse and passionate veterinary technician. He's worked with dogs for over twenty years and lives to improve the well-being of our canine companions. "See if you can find areas of tension and think about what you like. Do you like

a good neck massage? Shoulders? Back? Try massaging your dog in those same areas, then watch for a reaction." If a dog goes into a stretch, this communicates: *Yes, human! There!*

When working on the body, it's important to massage each side equally. For canines, the triceps area is usually a great place to start. This muscle controls the flex of a dog's leg, and dogs use it much more than humans do. Observing how your dog walks is also important. How is their posture? Are they favoring any particular area, limping, or walking gingerly? By rubbing all areas of our dogs, we can also discover growths that may need to be addressed by a veterinarian. "But just be warned," says Rukavina, "once a dog knows about the wonders of a great massage, she will keep coming back for more."

Emma

154

Become a Canine Therapist

WITH HELP FROM CHI CHI, CERTIFIED THERAPY DOG AND
2018 AMERICAN HUMANE HERO DOG, @CHICHIRESCUEDOG

It's a few days before Christmas, and I'm at the airport. Kids are crying. People are rushing around. There are lost bags and potential delays and germs and it's stressful. But then I see it—a bulldog sitting in the terminal next to a sign that reads, "Please, come pet me!" Cue the heavenly angel choir sound effects—it's a therapy dog! I hurry over for a free two-minute session with the therapist , where he prescribes four licks, five happy tail wiggles, and three adorable snorts. Next, the therapist rolls over so I can spend a couple of minutes scratching his belly (*clearly* to help *me* relax, obviously). I follow the doctor's orders, and boy is he talented, because soon the airport drama has disappeared, and I really do feel calmer. Happier! (Why do I pay my human therapist again?)

Dogs have a lot of natural gifts that make them fantastic therapists. They are nonjudgmental, gentle, and accepting of all types of people. Unlike special-assistance dogs, a therapy dog travels with her owner to spread happiness in schools, hospitals, hospices, airports, and even colleges during exam week. Therapy dogs come in all shapes and sizes—lots of rescue dogs become canine therapists.

Chi Chi (2014–2019), a quadruple amputee and winner of the 2018 American Humane Hero Dog Award, was a golden retriever and renowned canine therapist. After she was found in a trash bag in South Korea, many didn't think she would survive. "When she first joined our family, she was still healing from having portions of all four of her legs amputated and was understandably untrusting of people, given the abuse she had suffered. We focused on providing her with a loving and safe home, and she slowly started to trust people," says Elizabeth Howell, Chi Chi's human. Soon

Chi Chi heading off to work

the golden retriever started to do more than trust people; she was helping people! With four prosthetic legs and her wagging tail, Chi Chi set off to live the rest of her years as a canine therapist.

Chi Chi and Howell visited elementary schools and libraries, lending a furry and nonjudgmental ear to children while they practiced reading. They adventured to rehabilitation centers and veterans' hospitals to meet others with disabilities, inspiring new human friends to never give up. Chi Chi played with people at retirement homes and provided uncon-ditional love to patients in Alzheimer's clinics. Most importantly, Chi Chi created joy in rooms that didn't always see a lot of joy. "The most rewarding thing about having a therapy dog was seeing the impact our dog had on people. She had an ability to know what people need and provided that to them—encouragement, love, compassion, joy," says Howell. Stressed hospital staff, family members, and busy caretakers also always benefited from Chi Chi's visits.

Of course, as a certified canine therapy team, you and your pup won't just improve the lives of other people, you'll improve your own lives, too. Is your dog kind to everyone—and I mean *everyone*—no matter what? Is she constantly making friends with strangers? If so, your pooch has an important role in this world! If you're still putting off that official canine therapy degree, you can still help your dog help others. Whether you simply slow down on walks so your dog can meet more humans, or you bring your four-legged bundle of joy along to light up a boring morning spent at the laundromat, never underestimate your pup's special power to turn someone else's morning into a pretty wonderful day

"Chi Chi's ability to leave her past behind, forgive, and share her love was one of her most impactful lessons." –Elizabeth Howell

Take a DNA Test

WITH HELP FROM RYAN BOYKO, CEO AND COFOUNDER OF EMBARK

When you have your dog's DNA tested, you might assume that you are only trying to confirm that yes, your energetic and wild shelter dog from Brentwood, Tennessee, *is* a rare African Basenji. At least, that's what I thought I was doing.

I ordered the test, swabbed the inside of Bette's cheeks, sent her saliva sample back to be analyzed, then waited for Embark's scientists to tell me what type of dog I had. (A Basenji, of course.) Days passed and I received multiple updates from the lab. First, the scientists were delving into Bette's saliva cells, pulling out all of her doggy DNA. (Whoa. That's cool!) After purifying the DNA, they amplified it almost a million times. A week later, geneticists were observing more than 200,000 genetic addresses in Bette's genome and pulling information from all seventy-eight of her chromosomes. They were even using robots! It all sounded very high tech but maybe not necessary to confirm that, yes, Bette comes from a long line of distinguished African Basenjis. Just look at her almond-shaped eyes, chestnut red-and-white coat, curled tail, and untamed personality. Total Basenji! A few weeks later, Bette's breed results arrived in my inbox. My heart raced with excitement as I opened the email and clicked on the video. Uplifting piano music began to play as they revealed that Bette is a . . . wait? What? This is baloney!

As it turns out, I'm not the only human who has been confused by their doggy's DNA test results. Most humans see a large black-and-tan dog and suspect: Rottweiler. But Labs can carry the gene for a black-and-tan coat, too. Lots of humans see a low and long body type and suspect that Giuseppi is a Dachshund, but small poodles can also have the genetic variant for that body

shape. And it's easy to see a wire coat and think "terrier," but that coat can also come from a Shih Tzu. Basically, recessive genes cause a lot of dogs to not look exactly like you'd imagine.

"Could I maybe still have a Basenji?" I asked Ryan Boyko, the CEO and cofounder of Embark, hoping the results were somehow incorrect and that I still had an animal that came from the wild plains of Africa. One whose ancestors would have been friends with Nala on Pride Rock. He explained that it was very unlikely. Although Embark does leave a little room for error, there were not a lot of Basenjis in America just running around. The people who do have them are likely breeding them very carefully.

If there was anyone to trust with Bette's genetics, it was Boyko and the team of Embark scientists. An official research partner of Cornell University College of Veterinary Medicine, Embark's mission is to advance canine-health research and increase the longevity and vitality of dogs. Through its research-grade DNA genotyping platform, Embark helps support responsible breeders and enables mixed-breed owners to learn about their dog's breed ancestry, health, and more. Their DNA test analyzes more genetic information than any other dog DNA test available. So, they aren't just taking guesses over there.

Before starting Embark, Boyko and his cofounder (and brother) Adam Boyko traveled the world, studying dogs in forty countries on every inhabitable continent. Boyko is basically a talking encyclopedia of canine knowledge, filled with the history, traits, and health particulars of the domestic dog. Inspired by the dog-human relationship, Boyko overflows with interesting facts; for example, the only country in the world that doesn't have any dogs is the island nation of Maldives, located in the Indian Ocean. He also told me that the ancestor to modern dogs ("proto-dogs") probably began separating from other wolves more than 20,000 years ago, and that by 15,000 years ago, man's best friend was part of human society and spreading around the world. He talked about how dogs were buried in tombs with the ancient Egyptians and with the Incas in Peru. Ancient cave drawings in the Saudi desert illustrate the first human-dog relationship (the carvings show humans and dogs connected with leashes). When you look at the other animals that were available to domesticate and befriend at that time, the *wolf* might not have been the most obvious choice. So, this really shows how dogs felt about us, too. We didn't just pick them for companions. They picked us, too. Dogs and humans have evolved together. Today, we are one of the most successful interspecies partnerships in the world.

Embark can test your dog for more than 350 breeds—including wolf, coyote, dingo, and "village dog" ancestry. But soon I understood that doing a doggy DNA test was about a lot more than finding out whether Bette is a Basenji. Not only do her results help me learn more about my dog's health, but by contributing Bette's DNA to Embark, I am also contributing to scientific research that will help improve the lives of our furry friends everywhere. The more dogs that contribute DNA, the more scientists can learn. Each pup tested brings Embark closer to their mission of ending preventable disease in dogs. You might even find your dog's relatives. I found two of Bette's immediate family members, and one of them, a canine named Piglet, shares her beautiful smile! Plus, now when people ask me, "What kind of dog is that?" I can say with confidence that I have an *extremely* rare Cattle Dog-Chow Chow-German Shepherd-Rottweiler-Lab-Boxer-Alaskan Klee Kai-Miniature Schnauzer-Siberian Husky mix!

What kind do you have?

Be Blessed by the Divine

Every year on October 4th, humans celebrate the Feast Day of Saint Francis of Assisi, the patron saint of animals. Saint Francis encouraged humans to live in harmony with all living creations—especially the big, slobbery, cuddly, fluffy creations. On this special day, many churches hold a ceremony called the "Blessing of the Animals." Whether you have a Great Dane the size of a small pony or a Yorkie the size of a guinea pig (or if you just have a guinea pig), churches around the world open their doors and lawns to our nonhuman brothers and sisters, encouraging us to give thanks for the wonderful gift of animal friends. As the prayer is offered, dogs are gently sprinkled with holy water. Check community church calendars in your area for services open to canines. If you don't think your furry friend will enjoy a church crowd or receiving a blessing from a stranger, PETA (People for the Ethical Treatment of Animals) offers a DIY phone blessing with a priest. You can call 1-833-ASSISI-1 to receive a recorded blessing for your animal any day of the year. And may your life be filled with treats and belly rubs!

Kip

Become an AKC Canine Good Citizen

Of course your dog is a good boy, but is he a good neighbor? Forget the tricks, scent work, and agility training; the American Kennel Club "Canine Good Citizen" test and training program focuses on good manners, socialization, and responsible dog ownership. A Canine Good Citizen must pass a ten-step test that proves he or she can follow rules, respect the rights of others, and not overly react to the world around them. Through hours of training and practice, dogs learn how to be comfortable with strangers, keep cool in a stressful crowd, and not freak out when you leave their side. For some dogs, becoming a Canine Good Citizen is a walk in the park. For other dogs, walking in the park is not easy. Bette and I have a lot more training to do before advancing beyond Canine Decent Citizen, but she does continue to shine in other important community roles, like Squirrel Patrol and Stick Collector.

These tests aren't always easy for dogs, but once you and your pooch receive that freshly minted CGC certificate, you'll feel more confident navigating the world together.

TEST 1: ACCEPTING A FRIENDLY STRANGER

A stranger will shake hands and share a conversation with the dog's human. A good canine citizen will not react, jump, or bark at the stranger.

TEST 2: SITTING POLITELY FOR PETTING

Dogs must be able to sit and receive a gentle pet from a human citizen.

TEST 3: APPEARANCE AND GROOMING

Dogs have their coat examined, and they must accept a gentle combing and ear inspection from a stranger.

Fawkes

Certificate of Recogniti

Baki & Praew

Has successfully passed all requiremts, and earned the AKC Ti

Canine Good Citiz

Fabia Feuerabendt, #59861

CANINE
GOOD
CITIZEN

CANINE GOOD CITIZEN

TEST 4: LOOSE LEASH WALKING

Good doggy citizens know the human is in control of the walk. This test demonstrates that your dog can walk with a loose leash. The test includes a right turn, a left turn, and an about-turn.

TEST 5: WALKING THROUGH A CROWD

Can your pooch keep her cool in a crowd? Dogs and handlers must pass and walk around several people. Dogs may not jump, panic, or show apprehension.

TEST 6: OBEYING COMMANDS

Can your dog sit, stay, and lie down on command? Canine Good Citizens must master all three.

TEST 7: COMING WHEN CALLED

Does your dog have selective hearing? In this test, dogs are tested on their ability to come when called from ten feet away.

TEST 8: REACTION TO ANOTHER DOG

Good citizens know how to respect the space of other four-legged citizens. This test challenges your leashed dog to stay relaxed around another leashed dog while the two handlers have a conversation.

TEST 9: REACTION TO DISTRACTION

How does your dog react to unexpected joggers, loud noises, and other distractions? Good Canine Citizens may become slightly startled by a commotion, but they cannot bark, lunge, or try to run away.

TEST 10: SUPERVISED SEPARATION

Can you leave your dog with a stranger for three minutes and run out of sight if need be? In this test, the evaluator asks, "Would you like me to watch your dog?" Humans must hand over the leash and go out of sight. Mild agitation is acceptable, but the dog should not bark, whine, or excessively pace.

Baki

The Canine Commitment: Make Fetch Happen

I used to think that if I wanted to give my dog the best life ever, I needed to spoil her with handmade designer sweaters from fancy pet boutiques, buy her the most advanced and high-tech dog toys, and treat her to brunch on upscale restaurant patios. Even though I knew Bette was clearly a canine, there was always a voice inside me that seemed to want to say—*She's just like a human! Must! Give! Human! Things!* But she is not a human, obviously! And thankfully so, because her non human traits make her such a wonderful companion.

I like how my dog slurps water from the tub when I take a bath after a long day, and how she gazes up at me like I am a culinary wonder when I'm eating popcorn for dinner. I like how she inspires me to roll my window down and enjoy my car ride, instead of rushing through my errands as quickly as possible. Bette has been my faithful moving buddy on crosstown relocations and my reliable copilot on cross-country moves. She sits on top of me when I think I need to be alone. Yes, she's my dog, and she inhabits some of my most intimate moments because

of it. She knows my smell, memorizes my habits, witnesses my at-home workout dance routines (bless her), and still greets me with unbounded enthusiasm when I walk through the door. My goal is to try to be as amazing as Bette thinks I am. And for me, this is about taking her on as many fabulous adventures as possible. But it's also about making time for the simple adventures that Bette loves. Like, playing fetch.

I realize playing fetch might not seem the most innovative way to end a book about the most inspiring dog adventures. But Bette loves fetch! I mean, she *really* loves fetch. She loves fetch so much she does not even need toys to play it. We have played fetch with small sticks, fetch with large sticks, even fetch with pathetic, little mulch-sticks! Playing fetch with Bette reminds me that with the right attitude, I do not need much to enjoy at least *one* simple pleasure every day. And in a world where there is constant pressure to achieve that perfect, social media–worthy adventure, I admire how Bette seems to be completely happy enjoying whatever she has around her. It reminds me to enjoy whatever I have around me, too. So, I try scheduling fetch with her a few times a week. In fact, we played yesterday. It was raining. But I launched the trusty stick into the air and when it hit the ground with a muddy splat, we both chased after it. With water spattering my calves, my socks soaked through, and my drenched mutt happily by my side, maybe *this* was the best adventure ever.

So, now it's your turn. What adventure will you prioritize with your dog? Cross-country road trips are exhilarating. The view on top of a mountain peak is unforgettable. Stand-up paddleboarding with your dog really is possible! Do it! Go! Don't wait until the timing is perfect! And while you're busy plotting new adventures, don't forget to also make time for the simple ones. You do not have to drive hundreds of miles to sit in the park with your dog and enjoy the sun on your face. Your canine does not need a passport to walk on a new trail or explore a new part of the city. There are many delights right outside the front door if we only remember to look every day: the wonder of a squirrel leaping from tree to tree, the smell of a bakery around the block, the wave of a friendly stranger walking his dog, a game of Frisbee on the beach. Each day is a gift none of us is promised. What will you and your pup do with yours?

_____'S TO-DO LIST

- [ ] GO FOR A SMELL WALK
- [ ] GO FOR A PACK WALK
- [ ] WALK IN THE WORLD'S LARGEST DOG WALK
- [ ] GO FOR A REEEEAAALLY LONG WALK
- [ ] WALK ON THE BEACH

- [ ] PLAY IN THE SNOW
- [ ] LEARN TO MUSH
- [ ] RUN A CANICROSS RACE
- [ ] GO SKIJORING
- [ ] GO BIKEJORING
- [ ] BECOME A SUP PUP
- [ ] JUMP OFF A DOCK

- [ ] LEARN TO SURF
- [ ] TRAIN LIKE A NAVY SEAL
- [ ] PLAY SEARCH-AND-RESCUE GAMES

- [ ] HIKE TO THE TOP OF THE HIGHEST MOUNTAIN
- [ ] ORDER ROOM SERVICE AT A FANCY HOTEL
- [ ] VISIT THE DOG CHAPEL
- [ ] GO BISCUIT TASTING
- [ ] HERD AN ANIMAL
- [ ] SNIFF FOR TRUFFLES
- [ ] STAY IN A BEAGLE-SHAPED HOTEL
- [ ] DIG WITHOUT GETTING INTO TROUBLE

- [ ] LEARN TO HOWL
- [ ] BECOME A NATIONAL PARK B.A.R.K. RANGER
- [ ] MAKE NEW FRIENDS
- [ ] GO ON A ROAD TRIP

- [ ] TAKE UNDERWATER PHOTOS
- [ ] LEARN TO PAINT
- [ ] HAVE A PHOTO SHOOT
- [ ] LEARN A DANCE MOVE
- [ ] GRADUATE FROM THE IVY LEAGUE
- [ ] SET A GUINNESS WORLD RECORD
- [ ] BECOME AN INFLUENCER
- [ ] RUN FOR OFFICE

- [ ] HAVE A DATE NIGHT
- [ ] HAVE A SPA DAY
- [ ] TRY A DOGA POSE
- [ ] GET A MASSAGE
- [ ] BECOME A CANINE THERAPIST
- [ ] TAKE A DNA TEST
- [ ] BE BLESSED BY THE DIVINE
- [ ] BECOME AN AKC CANINE GOOD CITIZEN

- [ ] _____
- [ ] _____
- [ ] _____

Acknowledgments

As I traveled and did research for this book, I had the fortune of meeting all sorts of amazing two- and four-legged friends who helped bring these adventures to life. A great big thank you to the humans who graciously shared their expertise, knowledge, stories, and photographs with me. It was wonderful and inspiring to connect with so many of you about our shared love of dogs.

Andres Monasterios, Natalie Sanchez, and their pack
Ryan Boyko and the Embark team
Seth Casteel and Nala
Alexandra Horowitz
Adele Ng and Whiskey
Kelly Lund and Loki
Jennifer Raffaeli and the sled dogs of Denali National Park
Alex Rossington and the Running with the Bears Team
Samantha Eastburn and Jack
Linda Torson and the DockDogs team
Jim Zelasko and his passion for high-flying dogs
Liz Gregg & her Girl Pack
Andrew and Kicker
Ryan Rustan and Sugar
Lisa Scolman
Mike Ritland
Pam Medhurst and her pack
Jessica Williams and her pack
Courtney Dasher and Tuna
Jenny Neuburger and her hounds

Angela Rapti and Jimmy
Aaron Beltran, Cythia Lee, and the amazing Corgi Con team
Craig McGill and Susan Elliott and their passion for wine dogs
Frenchie and the humans of Frenchie Winery
Nola Jones
Kelly Mayfield
Charles Lefevre and Mocha and Dante
Kayt Mathers
Rowan Jacobsen
Dennis J. Sullivan and Frances Conklin
Stephanie Archer and Gabbie, Deano, and Swagger
Kim Langevin
Linus Zetterlund and Kiba
Sylvia Schlautmann and Milow and Pablo
Amy Burkert
Jamie Sun and Xena
Yvonnee Dagger and Dagger (DogVinci)
Brooks Morrison
Mike Dempsey
Lukas Pratschker and Falco
Rosana Robić

James Farrar and Otto
Zachary Silver and the Yale Canine Cognition Center
Loni Edwards
Phyllis Mueller and Mayor Max II
Clive Wynne and Xephos
Jess Rona
Pam Blair
Gene Rukavina
Elizabeth Howell and Chi Chi
Bob Fugate
The Friends of Dog Mountain
Amanda Marcus, Christina Fernandez, and the Guinness World Records team
Jason Beaton and Kip
Janée Lookerse and Fawkes
Anna Gensler and Pip
Shelby P. Maggart and Moody and Luna
Tyla Charbonneau, McConkey & Salix Sully
Axelle Woussen
Carly Perkins, Basil & Henley
Erin and Finley Molloy

Thank you to my amazing editor Brittany McInerney and my agent David Doerrer, as well as April Whitney, Natalie Nicolson, Jon Glick, and the rest of the team at Chronicle Books. I'm grateful for your guidance and enthusiasm.

Thanks to my dad for always being my most reliable reader and cheerleader, and to my wonderful human family—Mom, Erisy, Tripp, Jenna, Rebecca, Paula for always loving me and Bette unconditionally (even when it isn't the easiest to do so).

Thank you to Bette, obviously.

And lastly, to my main human, Max. Thank you for loving me and rooting for me. I feel so lucky every single day. If Bette could write, I'm sure she would also want to thank you for being such a patient father figure. You and Oscar are our favorite adventure yet!

Photography Credits

About the Author

Fern Watt is the author of *Gizelle's Bucket List: My Life with a Very Large Dog.* The book has been published in nineteen languages and optioned for film. Her work has appeared in *the L.A. Times*, *BBC Network*, *Cosmopolitan*, *BuzzFeed*, and more. Originally from Nashville, Tennessee, she resides in Venice Beach, California, with her human and best dog friends, a mischievous mutt named Bette and a labradoodle named Oscar. Follow their adventures at @lfernwatt.